THE WORLD IN ONE DAY

THE WORLD IN ONE DAY

Written by
RUSSELL ASH

DORLING KINDERSLEY
LONDON • NEW YORK • MOSCOW • SYDNEY

A DORLING KINDERSLEY BOOK

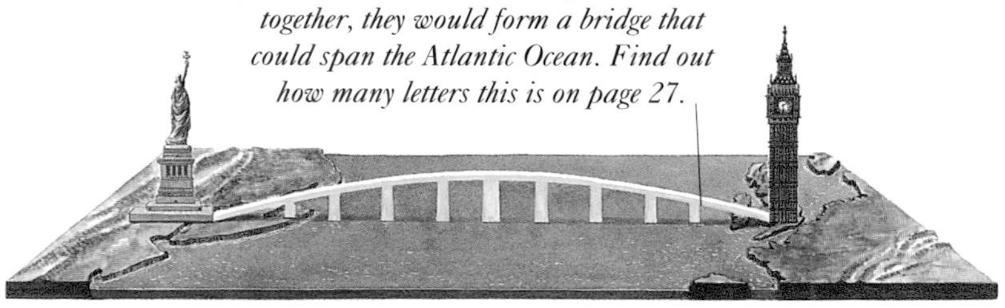

If all the letters sent in one day were stacked together, they would form a bridge that could span the Atlantic Ocean. Find out how many letters this is on page 27.

Senior Art Editor Dorian Spencer Davies
Art Editor Joanna Pocock
Project Editor Linda Sonntag
Managing Editor Sarah Phillips
Senior Managing Art Editor Peter Bailey
Production Charlotte Traill
DTP Designer Karen Nettelfield

First published in 1997
by Dorling Kindersley Limited,
9 Henrietta Street, London WC2E 8PS

Visit us on the World Wide Web at
http://www.dk.com

A CIP catalogue record for this book is available from the British Library.

ISBN 0-7513-5618-2

Reproduced in Great Britain by Dot Gradations Limited, Essex
Printed and bound in Italy by A. Mondadori Editore, Verona

The day featured throughout this book is not any particular one, but a typical day in the late 1990s. Of course, there may be certain days when fewer babies are born, or more rice is harvested, for example, but such figures, like all those that follow, are based on daily averages that have been calculated from authoritative statistics for longer periods.

CONTENTS

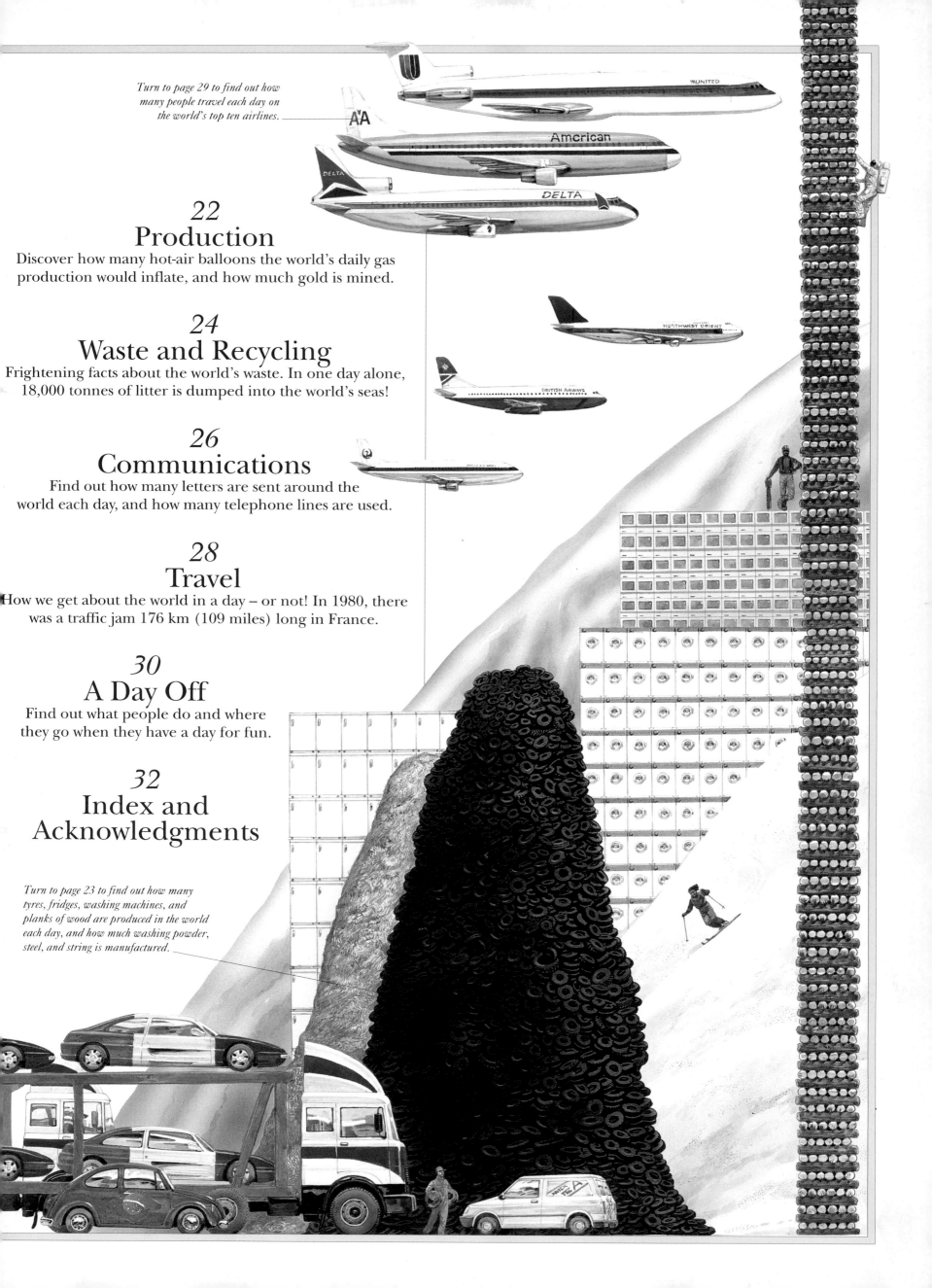

Turn to page 29 to find out how many people travel each day on the world's top ten airlines.

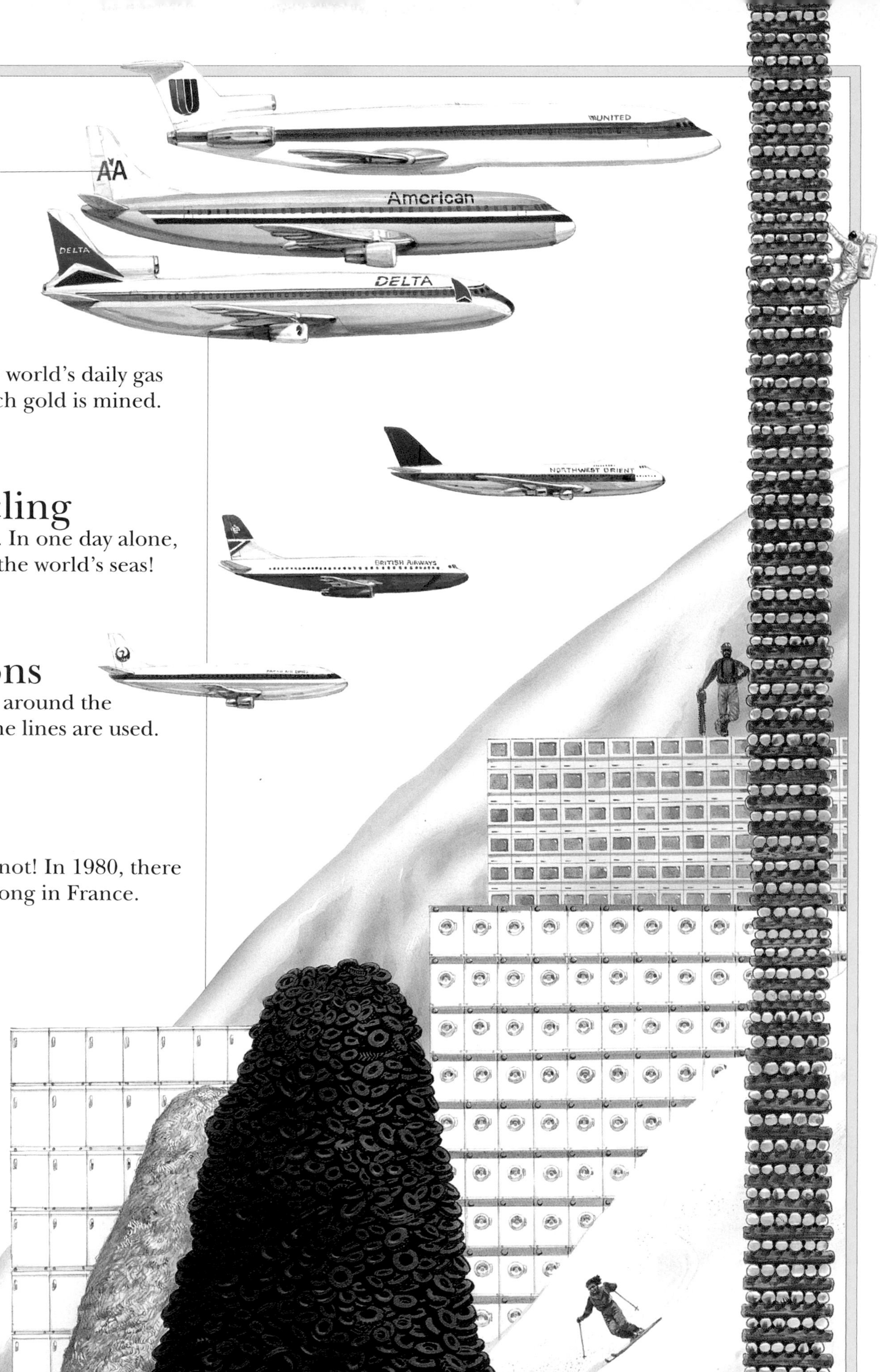

Turn to page 23 to find out how many tyres, fridges, washing machines, and planks of wood are produced in the world each day, and how much washing powder, steel, and string is manufactured.

A DAY AROUND THE WORLD

WHAT HAPPENS IN ONE DAY in the life of the world? In the next 24 hours, the world will spin once on its axis and travel more than 2.5 million km (1.5 million miles) in its orbit round the Sun. As they hurtle through space, 2.5 billion people will spend the day at work, and 1 billion children will go to school. But what else is going on? This book gives you the figures for many of the other things that happen in an average day, from how much water an elephant drinks and how many times a flea can jump, to how many potatoes are harvested and how much gold is made into false teeth. So fasten your seat belt as we lift off into the bizarre world of real facts. Enjoy it, and remember . . . tomorrow is another day.

"Beam me up!"

Every day, 98 astronauts train at the Kennedy Space Center, Cape Canaveral, USA.

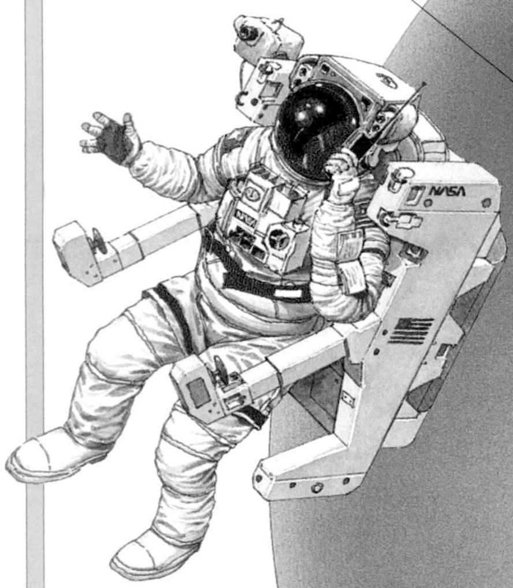

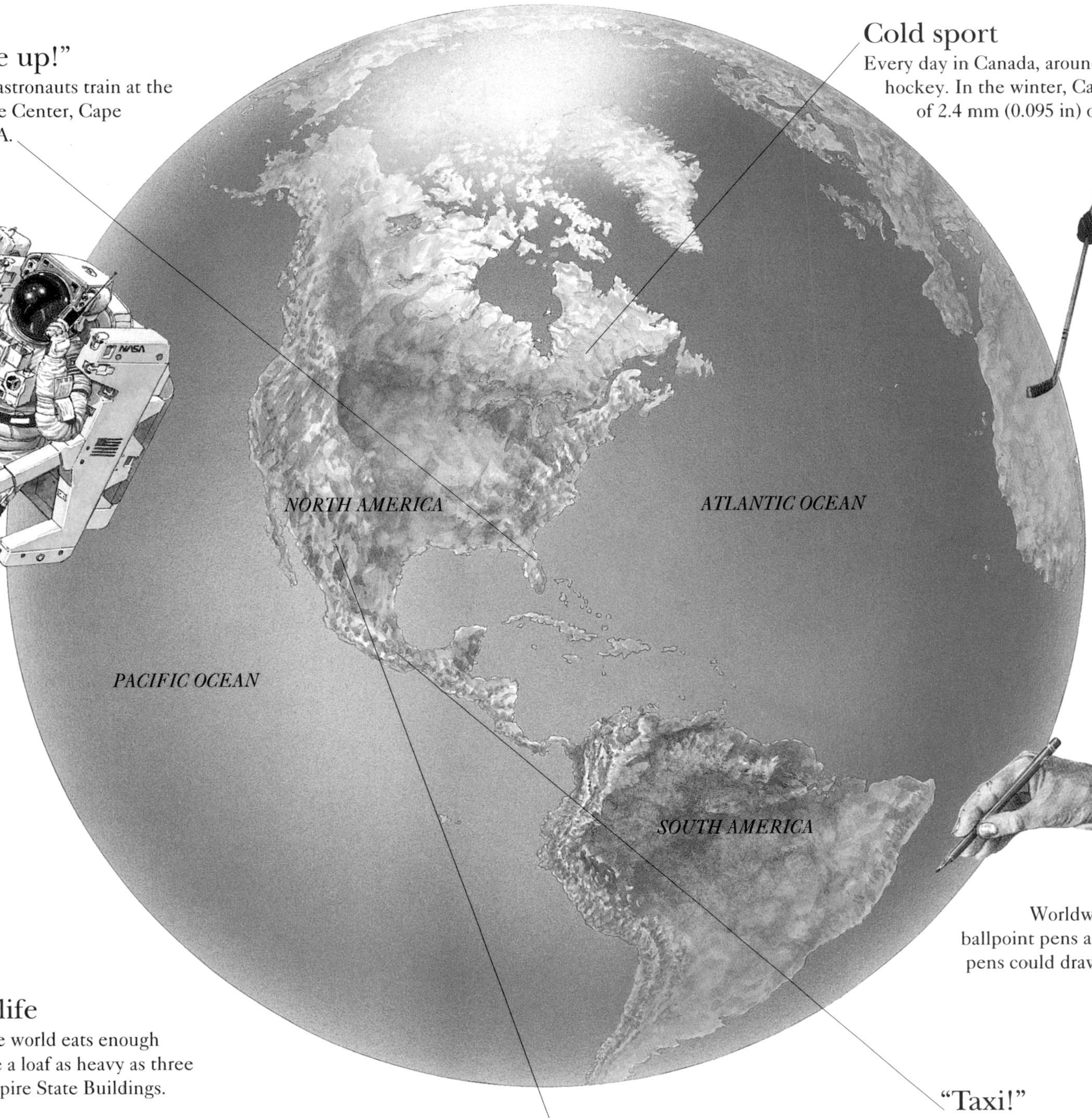

Cold sport

Every day in Canada, around 3,562 people play ice hockey. In the winter, Canada receives an average of 2.4 mm (0.095 in) of snow every day.

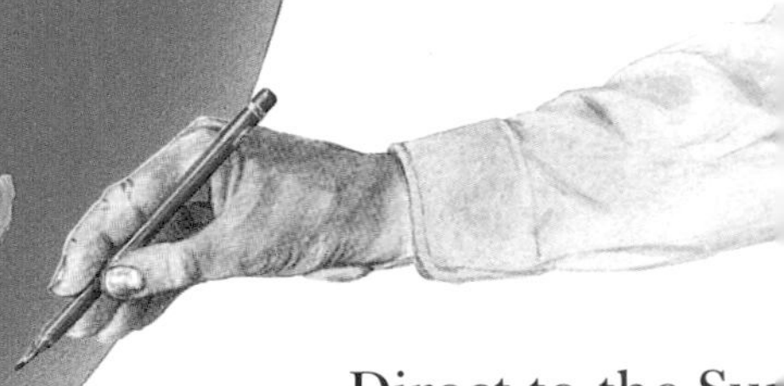

Direct to the Su

Worldwide, 15 million BiC Cryst ballpoint pens are sold every day. All thes pens could draw a line halfway to the Su

Bread of life

In one day, the world eats enough wheat to make a loaf as heavy as three Empire State Buildings.

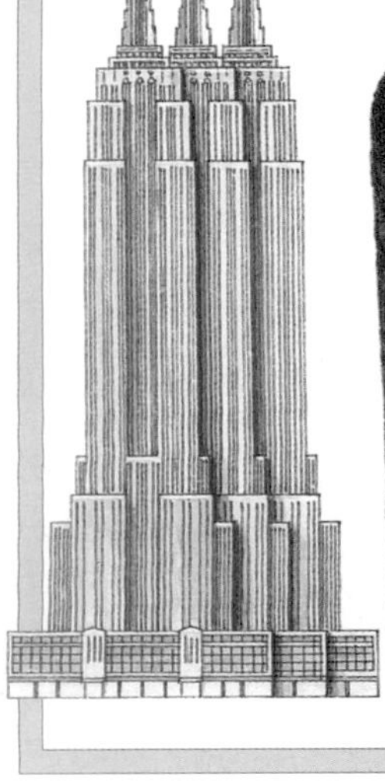

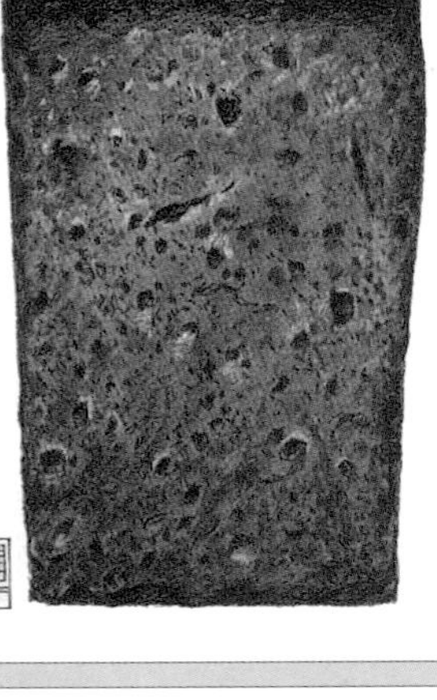

"America calling!"

Every day, Americans make 1.3 billion telephone calls, including 230 million long-distance calls and 6 million international calls.

"Taxi!"

Every day in Mexico City, 60,000 people work as taxi drivers. Mexico City has the biggest fleet of taxis in the world. It also has one of the world's worst air pollution problems. The day's traffic fumes are trapped by mountains surrounding the city.

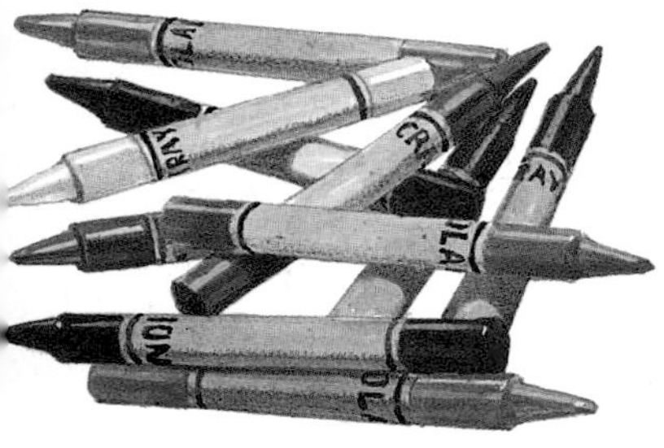

Waxing colourful

Crayola Crayons produces 5 million crayons worldwide every day. Children in the UK spend 3.5 million hours a day drawing and colouring.

Fishy story

Every day in Iceland, 15,000 people go to sea in fishing trawlers, or work in the fish-processing industry.

For better or worse

Every day in China, 26,000 couples get married. The average age for people to marry in China is thirty.

Military jobs

1.3 million people work every day in the armed forces of the Russian Federation. These include 460,000 in the army, 190,000 in the navy and 145,000 in the air force.

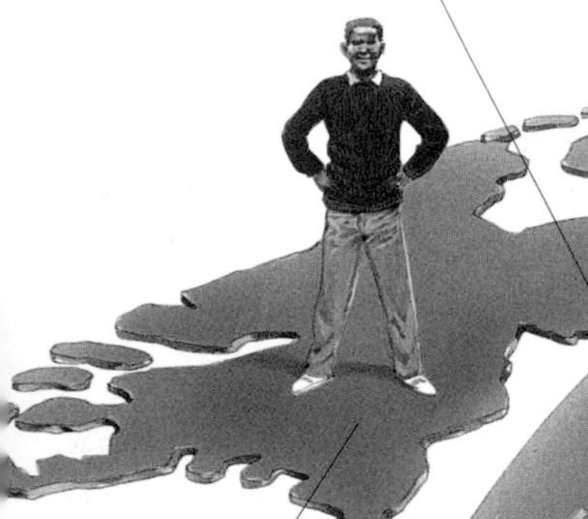

Feeling sheepish

The world's sheep yield 5,000 tonnes of wool a day. That's enough to make 15.5 million jumpers, one for each person in the Netherlands.

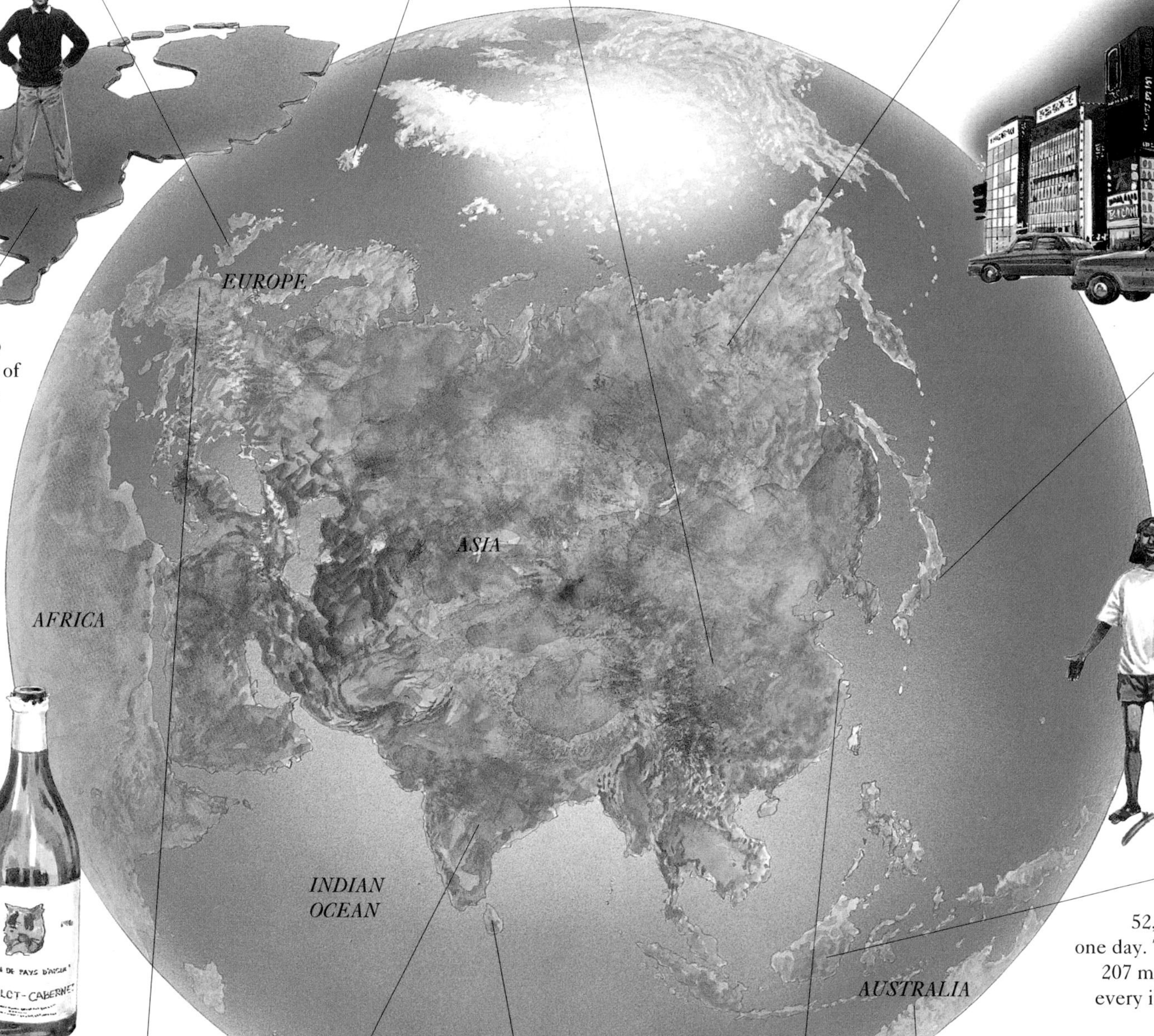

Booming city

Tokyo-Yokohama, in Japan, is the biggest continuous urban area, with a population of 28 million. Every day, the population here grows by 819 inhabitants.

Cottoning on

The world harvests 52,000 tonnes of cotton in one day. That's enough to make 207 million T-shirts – one for every inhabitant of Indonesia.

Drink of the gods

The French produce 15,000 tonnes of wine every day. That's 20 million bottles a day!

Flying kangaroo

Every day, 2,624 people work for Qantas, Australia's national airline company.

Snakes alive!

Every day in Sri Lanka, an average of two people are killed by poisonous snakes. Sri Lanka's most common killer snake is the saw-scaled, or carpet, viper, one of the most poisonous snakes in the world.

Steamy work

Every day, 1.6 million people go to work for Indian Railways, the biggest non-governmental employer in the world.

On their bikes

The people of Shanghai, in China, make 2.5 million bicycle trips every day. Shanghai also has the world's largest bicycle manufacturer, the Forever Bicycle Factory, which makes 4,500 bikes every day.

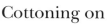

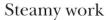

PLANET EARTH

SINCE IT CAME INTO BEING around 4,600 million years ago, Planet Earth has continued to evolve every day. Heat from the Earth's core forces molten material to bubble to the surface in volcanoes. The plates that form the hard outer layers of the Earth grind against one another. The enormous pressure they exert pushes mountain ranges gradually higher, pulls the continents apart, and causes tremors and earthquakes. Wind, ice, and water wear away at rock, creating a landscape that is slowly changing day by day.

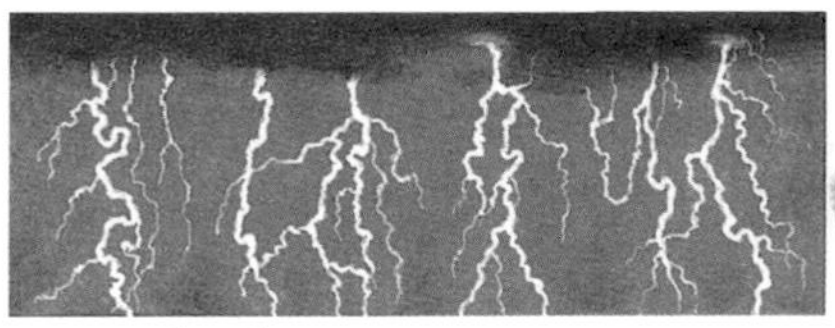

In a flash

Lightning strikes somewhere on Earth 100 times a second. A lot of it zigzags straight into the sea or hits icecaps or huge uninhabited areas of land, so the chances of getting struck by lightning are quite remote. The odds are higher in the tropics, where 3,200 electric storms light up the sky every 12 night hours.

Powering Nicaragua by tropical storms

Lightning power

If the power of all the tropical storms that take place in 24 hours could be harnessed, it would be equal to a full year's electricity consumption in a small country like Nicaragua.

Nightly fireworks

Stromboli is a volcano that has been active every day for thousands of years. The Ancients called it the Lighthouse of the Mediterranean, because it produces a spectacular display of sizzling bombs and red fountains of lava against the night sky.

Volcanic energy

The energy released in one day by the eruption of Mount Tambora was reckoned to be 16,000 megatons – 800,000 times as powerful as the Hiroshima atom bomb.

Mount Stromboli could go on erupting for hundreds of years before it becomes dormant and finally extinct.

Great balls of fire

Mount Vesuvius erupted in AD 79. Lava exploded into the air as ash and buried Pompeii. Its inhabitants were suffocated by poisonous gases. Ash then mixed with rain to create hot mud flows (lahars), which buried Herculaneum in just one day. The lethal lahars would have kept up with a modern Italian trying to escape on a moped.

"I'm burning rubber! Hey! Get this lahar off my tail!"

The Bering Glacier in the Arctic began to retreat in the 1980s, raising fears about global warming. In 1993 it started to advance again.

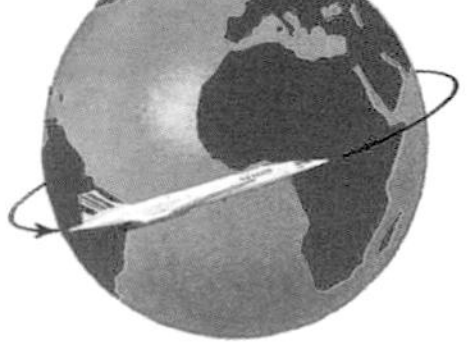

Earth in orbit

Planet Earth spins so fast on its axis that a person standing on the Equator is actually travelling at 1,670 kmh (1,038 mph) – the speed of Concorde – without moving at all.

Jupiter	Saturn	Neptune	Uranus	Earth	Mars	Pluto	Mercury	Venus
9h 55m	10h 39m	16h 7m	17h 14m	24h	24h 37m	6 days 9h	58 days 14h	244 days

How long is a day?

A day on Earth lasts 24 hours, but a day on Venus lasts eight Earth months, because Venus spins so slowly. Jupiter spins so fast that a day flashes by in under ten hours. An Earth watch would have to lose two minutes an hour to keep time on the Moon.

The ice advances

Most glaciers are slow movers. They grind forward by about 2 m (6 ft) a day. The Bering Glacier in the Arctic is an exception. It advances an astonishing 91 m (300 ft) every day. It could transform a large back garden into a skating rink overnight.

Cosmic dust

Every day 110 tonnes of cosmic dust – debris from outer space – enters the Earth's atmosphere. If it could all be shovelled into one heap, it would be as big as a two-storey house.

ANIMALS

A LOUD CHORUS of birdsong shakes the animal kingdom from its slumber as the first rays of the Sun touch the treetops. The animals' day centres around key survival activities: defending territory, hunting or foraging for food, and feeding young. Mammals, birds, and winged insects also spend time grooming to keep their bodies clean and healthy. Monkeys and apes groom each other to cement friendships; a cow may indulge in 180 bouts of grooming in one day!

Hummingbird Up to 5,400 wingbeats a minute.

Bat Up to 1,200 wingbeats a minute.

Sparrow 600 wingbeats a minute.

Butterfly Up to 640 wingbeats a minute.

Swift 360 wingbeats a minute.

Stork 180 wingbeats a minute.

In a flap

Most birds, insects, and bats need to beat their wings rapidly in order to stay in the air. A hummingbird's wings beat so quickly you can hardly see them.

Pygmy shrew Up to 2 million heartbeats a day.

Mouse 720,000 heartbeats a day.

Elephant 43,200 heartbeats a day.

Frog 43,200 heartbeats a day.

Heartbeats

Astonishingly, all mammals other than humans have around 800 million heartbeats in a lifetime. An elephant's heart beats 20–30 times a minute, so it will have "used up" its heartbeats after about 50 years. At the other end of the scale, a pygmy shrew's heart beats 900–1,400 times a minute; its lifespan is about 1.5 years.

Rabbit 288,000 heartbeats a day.

Hedgehog 432,000 heartbeats a day.

Hedgehog hibernating 4,320 heartbeats a day.

On the run

Animals run to escape predators and to chase prey. This race of slowcoaches and speedy creatures shows how far animals could travel if they were able to sprint along at their top speeds for a whole 24 hours.

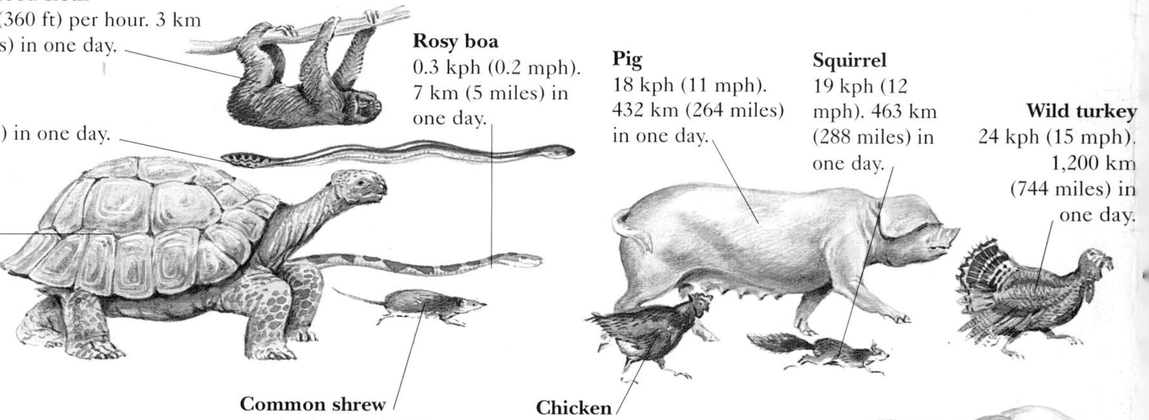

Three-toed sloth 110 m (360 ft) per hour. 3 km (2 miles) in one day.

Rosy boa 0.3 kph (0.2 mph). 7 km (5 miles) in one day.

Pig 18 kph (11 mph). 432 km (264 miles) in one day.

Squirrel 19 kph (12 mph). 463 km (288 miles) in one day.

Wild turkey 24 kph (15 mph). 1,200 km (744 miles) in one day.

Yellow-bellied sea snake 3 kph (2 mph). 77 km (48 miles) in one day.

Giant tortoise 370 m (1,214 ft) per hour. 8,880 m (29,136 ft) per day.

Common shrew 5 kph (3 mph). 116 km (72 miles) in one day.

Chicken 15 kph (9 mph). 348 km (216 miles) in one day.

Animal appetites

For some creatures, eating is hard work. The African elephant spends about 18 hours out of 24 feeding and drinking. The giant anteater chomps its way through 30,000 ants in one day, and the sperm whale swallows a whole tonne of squid. Others just sit back and let it happen. Moles feed on unsuspecting bypassers that drop into their tunnels.

Vampire bat Drinks two tablespoons of blood every day, the equivalent of half its own bodyweight.

Mole Eats its own weight (50–80 g/ 2–3 oz) of food every day.

Bull elephant Eats 227 kg (500 lb) of foliage in one day. Drinks 80–160 litres (18–35 gallons) of water.

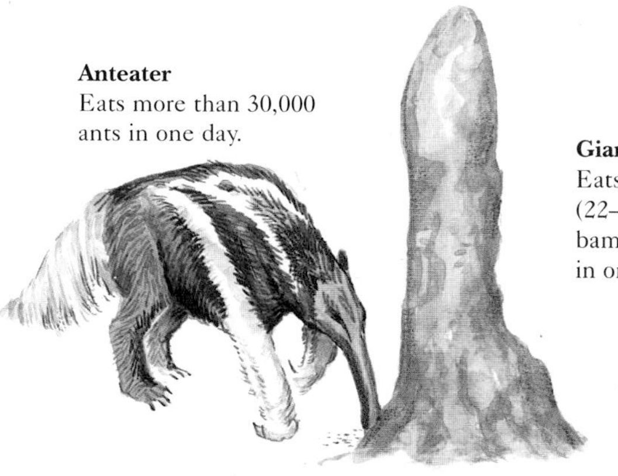

Anteater Eats more than 30,000 ants in one day.

Giant panda Eats 10–45 kg (22–99 lb) of bamboo shoots in one day.

Blue whale Absorbs five tonnes of krill (tiny crustaceans) in one day.

BEES' WORLD

As the Sun rises, a beehive starts to buzz with activity. The youngest workers clean the hive. After three days, they are promoted to feeding the larvae. After ten days, their job is to build the comb, and after 16 days, they start filling the comb with pollen and nectar. After 20 days, they guard the entrance of the hive, and finally they leave the hive to gather nectar. The queen bee lays 1,500 eggs a day.

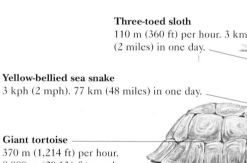

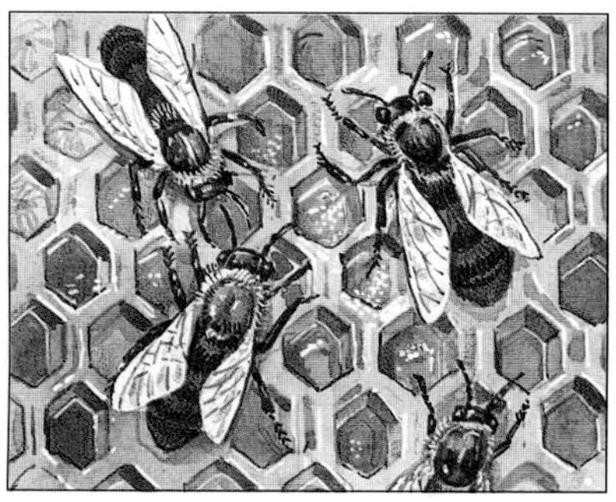

PLANTS

WITHOUT PLANTS, THERE WOULD BE no life on Eart. Plants produce oxygen, which all creatures need to breath to convert food into energy. Their fruits, leaves, and seeds us food and medicines. Their fibres are woven into clothe. Their juices give us drinks and dyes. Trunks and branches provide shelter, fuel, and material for furniture and tools. S we have identified 500,000 plants, and still more await discovery. Yet large areas of natural vegetation are disappea. Every day, 36,000 hectares (89,000 acres) of tropical rainfor are destroyed. But just one Amazonian Brazil nut tree can produce more nutritious food than can be cultivated on the land that is cleared when the tree is felled.

Plant growth

Plants harness energy from the Sun's rays, turning it into glucose, which they use to grow. This process is called photosynthesis. A large rainforest tree can produce 1.5 kg (3 lb) of pure glucose in one day, using just sunlight and water. Some plants, like those on the left, grow very quickly. Compared with these plants, even the fastest-growing trees seem to grow slowly. Some of the slowest-growing plants are lichens (see bottom right), which can take a century to grow just 2.5 cm (1 in)!

Morning

The flowers of morning glory las day. They open in the morning a and die towards evening. Plants responding to the number of hours of in a day. A light-sensitive pigme leaves sends a hormone sign flowerbuds, triggering them t

Giant bamboo
A native of Burma, the giant bamboo can grow an astonishing 46 cm (18 in) a day. Bamboo is technically a grass. Its stems are used for making buckets, rafts, and chopsticks. In India and Southeast Asia, the bamboo harvest is turned into 4,800 tonnes of paper a day.

Giant kelp
Giant kelp is a huge seaweed found in the coastal waters of California. It grows up to 45 cm (18 in) per day. Fronds of kelp form underwater forests, and can reach 100 m (328 ft), making it the tallest plant in the world.

Callie grass
Callie grass grows 15 cm (6 in) in one day.

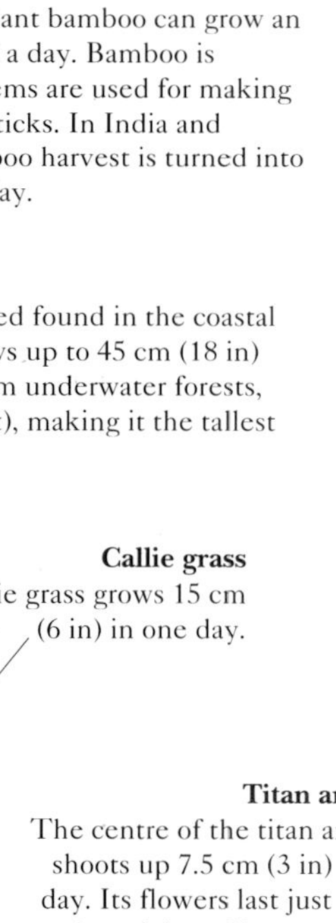

Titan arum
The centre of the titan arum shoots up 7.5 cm (3 in) in a day. Its flowers last just one day, giving off a stench of rotting flesh. In its native Sumatra, the titan arum is known as the "corpse flower".

Eucalyptus deglupta
This eucalyptus is the world's fastest-growing tree. It can spurt 2.5 cm (1 in) in a day. One specimen in New Zealand reached 10.6 m (35 ft) in 15 months.

Powering the USA by hurricane

America by storm

In one day, a hurricane could produce enough energy to replace the whole of the United States' electricity supply for nine months.

A day's work for the Sun

Every day the Sun beams four trillion kilowatt hours of energy to Earth. This recycles Earth's water by evaporation, causes winds, waves, and ocean currents, and is used in photosynthesis.

Squeaky clean

Enough rain falls to Earth every day for each one of its inhabitants to have a bath every five minutes.

Small World

Biosphere 2 is a huge greenhouse built in Arizona. Inside the Biosphere are areas of farmland, rainforest, desert, and even an ocean. This is the home of an experiment in global warming. Levels of carbon dioxide (CO_2) in Earth's atmosphere are rising. Scientists will steadily pump more CO_2 into Biosphere 2 in order to predict Earth's future.

Wet, wet, wet

If all the moisture in Earth's atmosphere fell as rain, it would produce 1,250 cu km (300 cu miles) of water. If all this rain fell in one day on the island of Manhattan, it would submerge it to a depth of 20,000 km (12,500 miles).

Solar energy

It would take 167,000 nuclear power stations to produce the amount of energy that the Sun beams down to Earth in one day.

When the wind blows

Erosion is the wearing away and removal of land surfaces by running water, wind, or ice. Erosion is greatest in sloping areas and areas of little or no surface vegetation. On the west coast of Mauritania near Nouakchott, prevailing easterly winds carry 696,000 tonnes of sand and dust from the Sahara Desert into the Atlantic Ocean every day.

Cold snout

The end of a glacier is called the snout. At the snout, the ice either melts as fast as it arrives, or the glacier calves – bits break off to form icebergs. Jakobshavn Glacier in Greenland discharges 20 to 30 million tonnes of ice a day to the fiord at its snout.

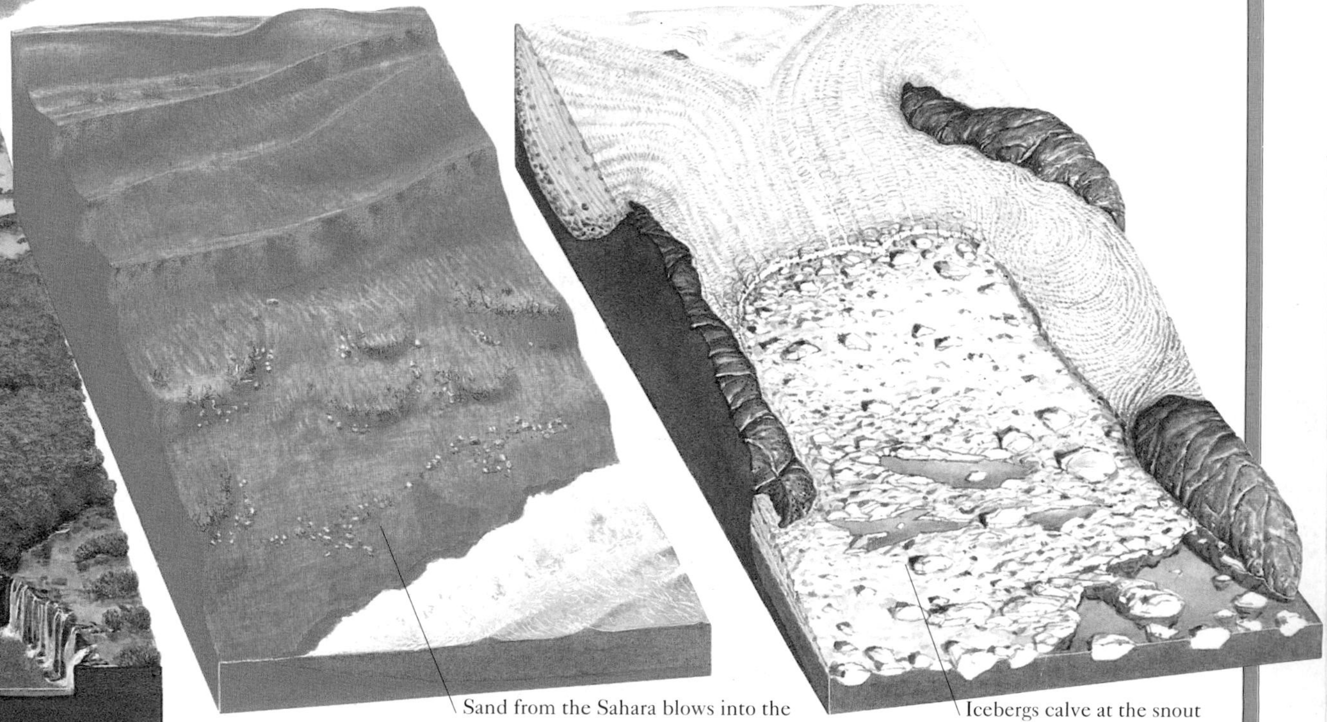

Sand from the Sahara blows into the Atlantic from the west coast of Africa.

Icebergs calve at the snout of Jakobshavn Glacier in Greenland.

A raging torrent

The Iguaçu Falls are a string of 275 waterfalls on the border between Argentina and Brazil, close to Paraguay. The water of the Iguaçu River cascades down spectacular drops of up to 70 m (230 ft). At times of peak flow, enough water passes over the Falls to fill six Olympic swimming pools every second. However, in some years rainfall is so slight that this great river can dry up completely, as it did in 1978.

The Earth moves

An earthquake happens when rocks move along faults. Earthquakes are especially powerful when the tectonic plates that form the Earth's outer layers move against one another. The Great African Rift Valley in Djibouti experiences dozens of earthquakes every day, indicating the continuous movement of the tectonic plates beneath Africa.

A Day to Remember

Up to your ears

The wettest day ever was 15 March 1952, when 190 cm (74 in) of torrential rain fell at Cilaos on the island of La Réunion in the Indian Ocean.

It drove them quackers

On 14 July 1953, golf ball-sized hailstones fell in a freak storm in Alberta, Canada. Powered by gale-force winds, they bashed to death 36,000 ducks.

Piste off

The biggest snowfall ever was recorded on 7 February 1963, when 198 cm (78 in) of snow fell at Mile 47 Camp, Cooper River Division, Alaska, USA.

Sunny side up

On 13 September 1922 the temperature in the shade at al'Aziziyah in the Libyan desert reached 57.8°C (136°F) – hot enough to fry an egg on a rock.

On the wing

Men who tried to fly like birds made the painful discovery that human arms are feeble compared to wings. Birds and bats fly by powerful flapping movements, interspersed with gliding. Insect flight muscles need to be warm to work properly, so a bumblebee has to bask in the sun or do shivering exercises before buzzing off.

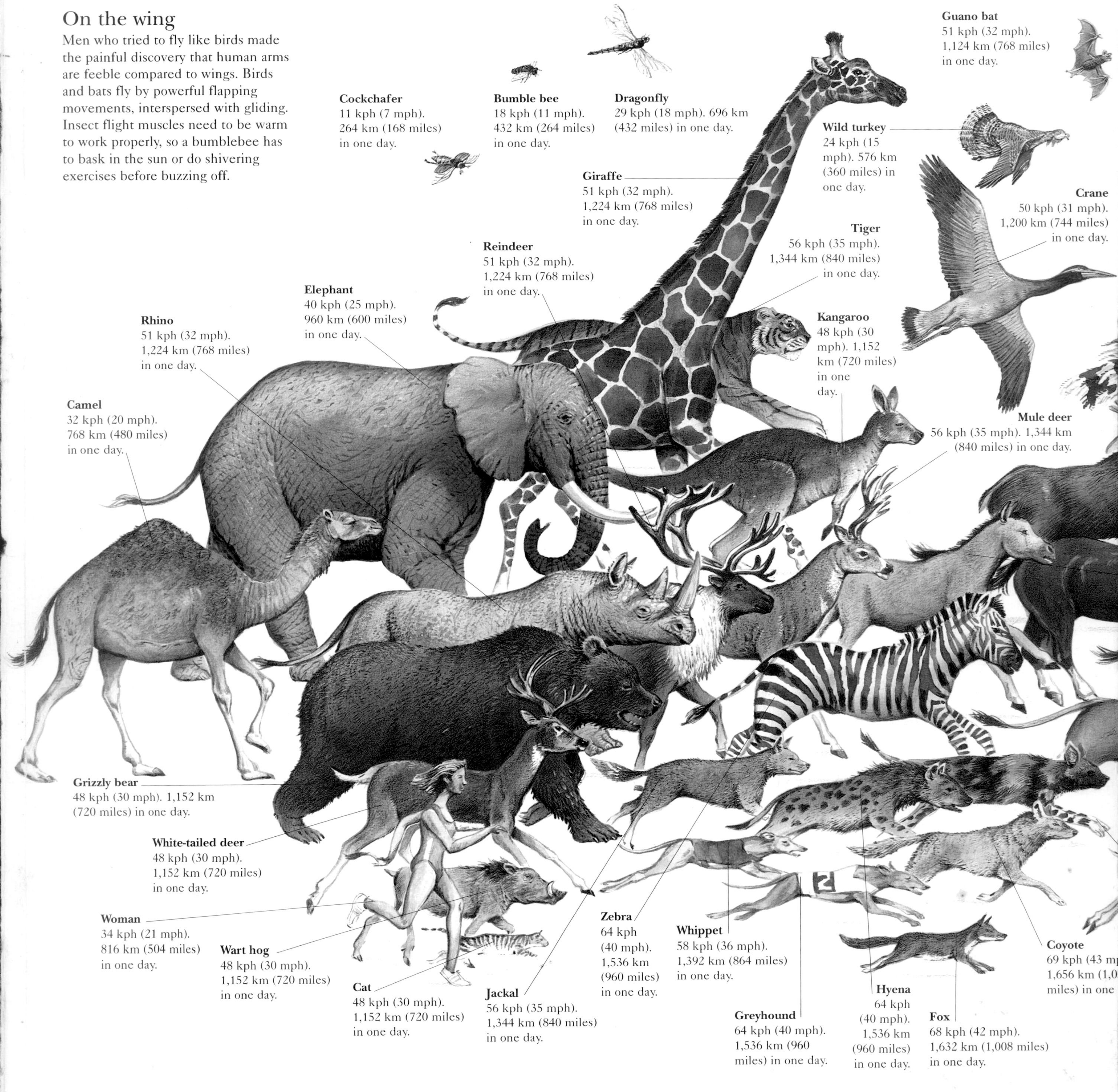

In the swim

Most animals – even sloths and moles – can swim in an emergency. But for many creatures, the water is their home. Fish swim by bending their bodies into S-shaped curves. Whales and dolphins undulate their bodies up and down. Penguins fly through the water, even though they can't fly in the air. Sea lions swim with their large, webbed forelegs, and seals swing the hind end of their bodies from side to side.

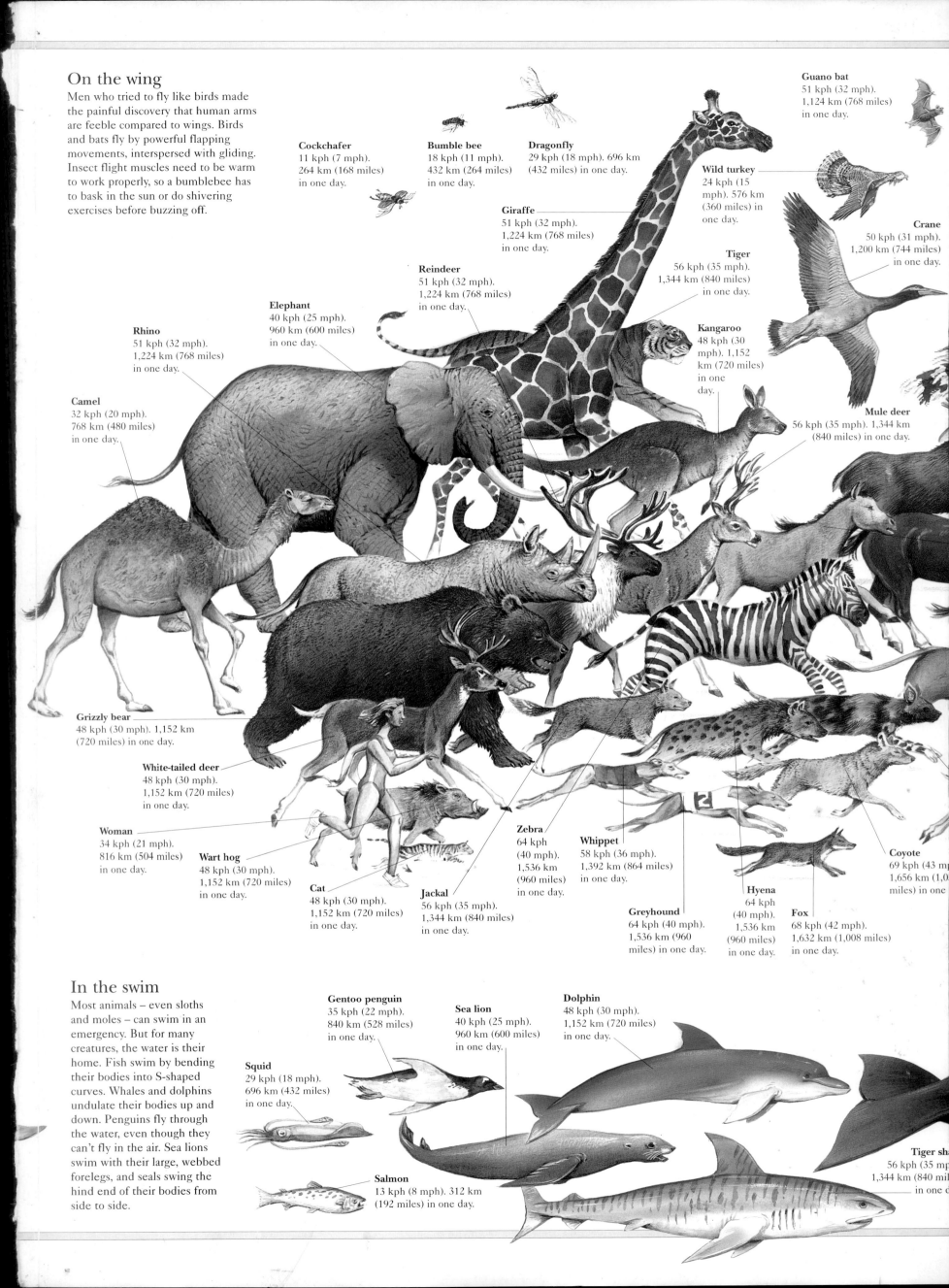

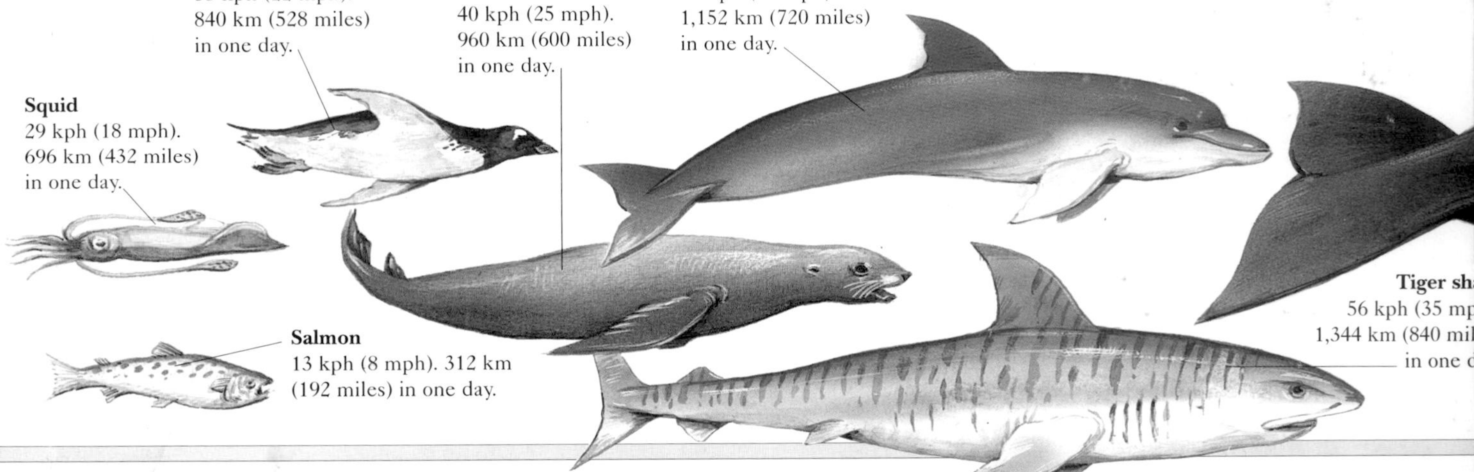

SMALL WORLD

The Royal Botanic Gardens at Kew, near London, UK, house 40,000 living plants, including a growing example of one in eight of all known flowers, and more than 6 million dried plants (nine out of ten of all species). This is the largest collection of plants in the world. Many of the plants grow in one of several greenhouses at Kew. The greenhouses recreate the conditions of different climates from around the world, ranging from hot desert to cold alpine. Many visitors to Kew feel as if they have travelled the globe in just one day.

Giant puffball

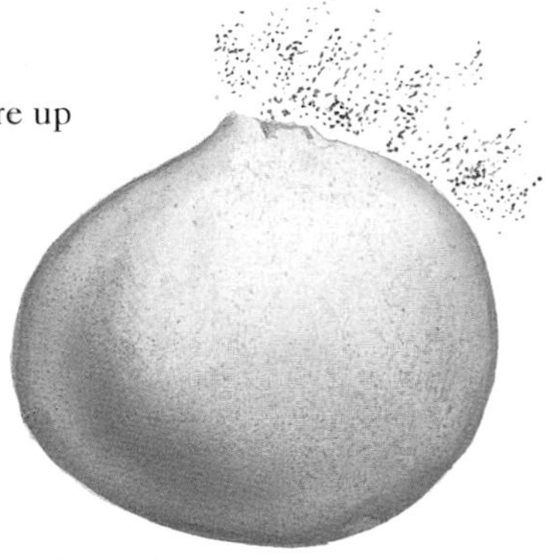

The giant puffball fungus can measure up to 2m (6.6 ft) in circumference, and weigh up to 20 kg (44 lb). If an animal or a raindrop strikes the fungus, spores (seeds) are puffed out of a hole in the top. In just one day, a giant puffball can release 7 billion spores.

Fairy ring

A toadstool springs from underground filaments called a mycelium. Some toadstools appear as if by magic, in a circle overnight, as the mycelia grows out from a central point. These formations are often called "fairy rings".

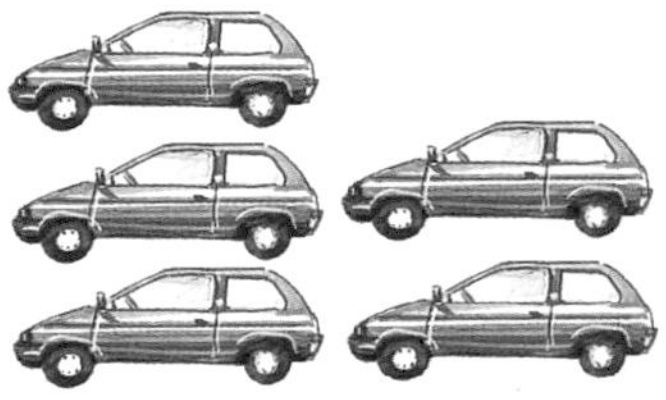

Diesel tree

The copaiba tree, which grows in the Amazon, contains an oil similar to diesel. It can produce 9 litres (2 gallons) of this oil every hour. So one tree could yield 218 litres (48 gallons) of fuel in one day, enough to fill the petrol tanks of five cars! Diesel trees are now being cultivated in Japan for their oil.

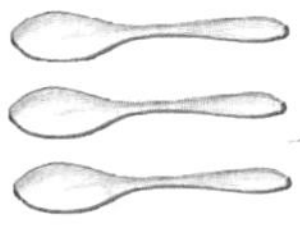

Petroleum nut

The petroleum nut tree, which grows in Borneo and the Philippines, produces a high-octane oil in its seeds. The seeds of one tree yield 53 litres (12 gallons) a year, which is about three teaspoonsful every day. The oil is burned in lamps, and was used by the Japanese during World War II to fuel tanks.

Rubber tree

When a cut is made in the bark of a rubber tree, a sticky white liquid called latex oozes out. Rubber trees flourish in the warm, moist climates of Malaysia, Indonesia, and Thailand. They produce 14,000 tonnes of rubber every day.

Oak

Oak trees live to a great age – one in Switzerland is thought to be around 930 years old. A mature oak tree draws 90 litres (20 gallons) of water out of the earth every day. Oak trees are very slow-growing, putting on only 1.4 mm (0.055 in) in one day.

Rampant growth

Tropical rainforest grows twice as fast as temperate oakwood. Every hectare of warm, wet rainforest produces 75 kg (165 lb) of lush new growth per day (67 lb per acre). Each hectare (2.5 acres) of rainforest contains 300 tonnes of 180 different species of tree, one tonne of plants, one tonne of earthworms, and 8 kg (18 lb) of birds.

Trumpet tree
Saplings of the trumpet tree growing on the rainforest floor shoot up towards the light at a rate of 7 mm (0.28 in) in one day.

Tasmanian cider gum
One of the fastest-growing of all trees, the cider gum (native to Tasmania) can grow 4 mm (0.16 in) taller every day.

Poplar
A poplar tree grows just over 3 mm (0.118 in) taller every day.

Bristlecone pine
The bristlecone pine grows very slowly, at only 0.009 mm (0.00035 in) a day. This tree is very long-lived. One specimen is believed to be 4,600 years old.

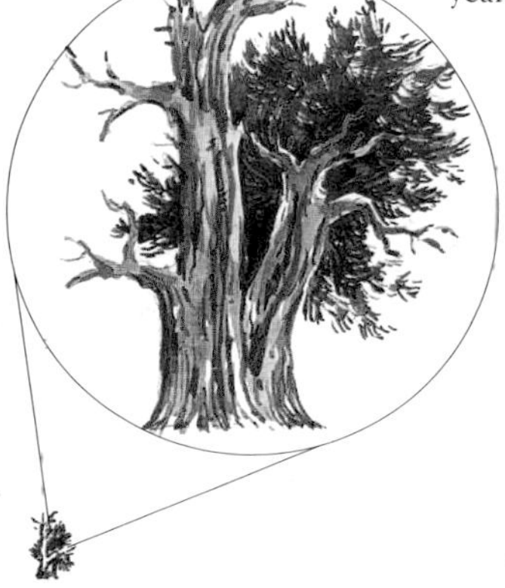

Lichens
Lichens are extremely slow growers, putting on 0.0025 mm (0.0001 in) a day.

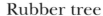

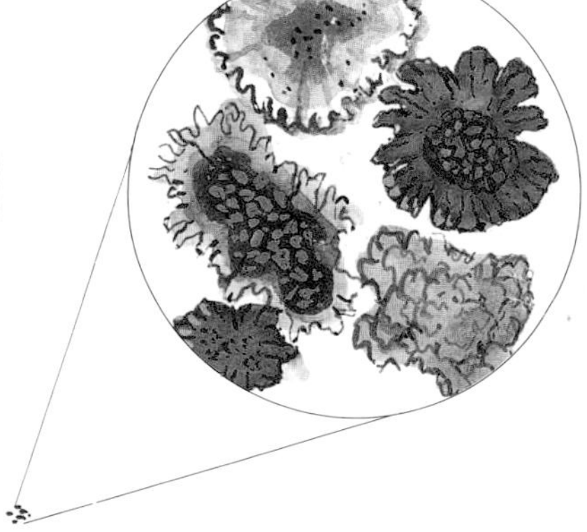

Sleepy creatures

Some animals sleep almost all day long, and others hardly sleep at all. The amount of sleep an animal needs depends partly on how it feeds. The sleepy koala bear has a low-energy diet of leaves, and snoozes for around 22 hours out of 24. The tiny shrew is a carnivore that has to feed almost constantly to survive, leaving precious little time for dozing.

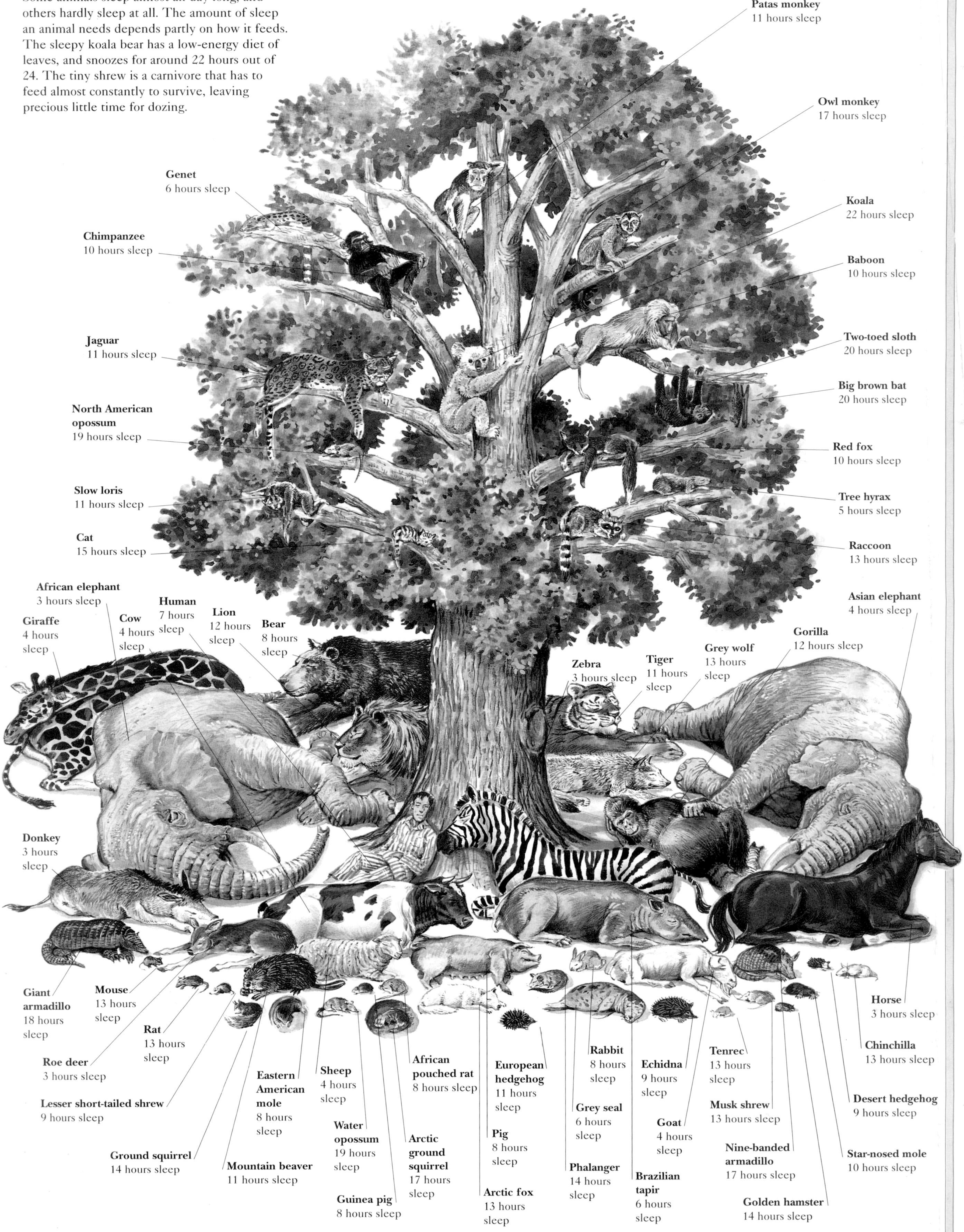

A Day to Remember

Quagga

The last quagga, a type of zebra, expired in Amsterdam zoo, Holland on 12 August 1883.

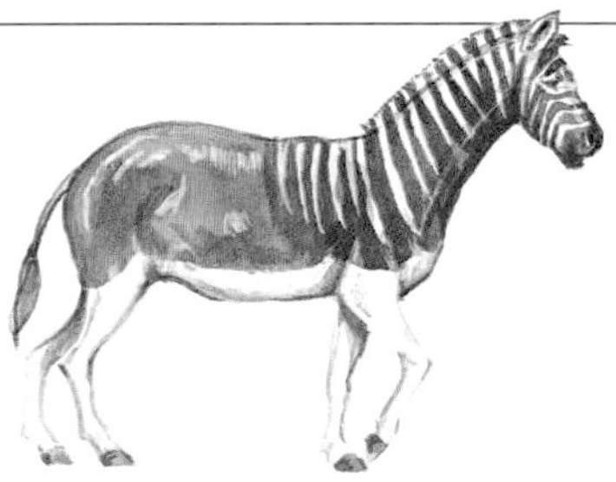

Great auk

The last surviving pair of great auks was killed on 4 June 1844 on Eldey Island, UK, for a collector.

Passenger pigeon

The last passenger pigeon was a 29-year-old bird called Martha. She died on 1 September 1914 at Cincinnati zoo.

Carolina parakeet

The last Carolina parakeet, a male called Incas, died of old age at Cincinnati zoo, USA, on 21 February 1918.

Energetic animals

Some animals have amazing stamina. The rhinoceros beetle can carry 850 times its own weight, while the Arctic tern migrates over a distance of 40,000 km (24,856 miles).

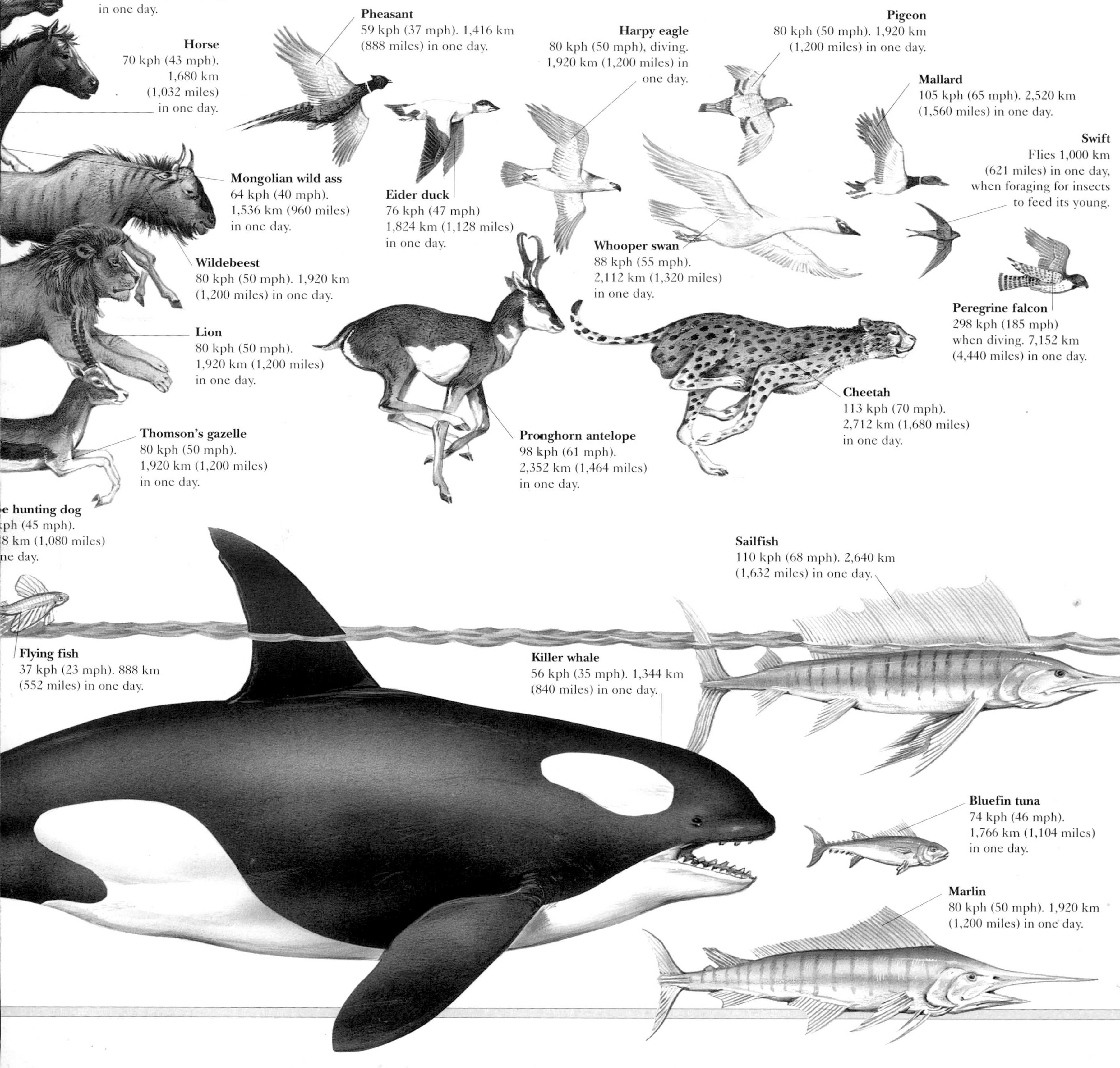

Mole
Moles can dig at a rate of 10 m (33 ft) per hour, so a mole putting in a 24-hour day could dig a tunnel 240 m (787 ft) long.

Chamois
A chamois can climb 4,000 m (13,123 ft) in one hour. In a day it could ascend ten Mount Everests.

Spider
A spider takes up to an hour to spin a web, so in one day it could spin 24 webs.

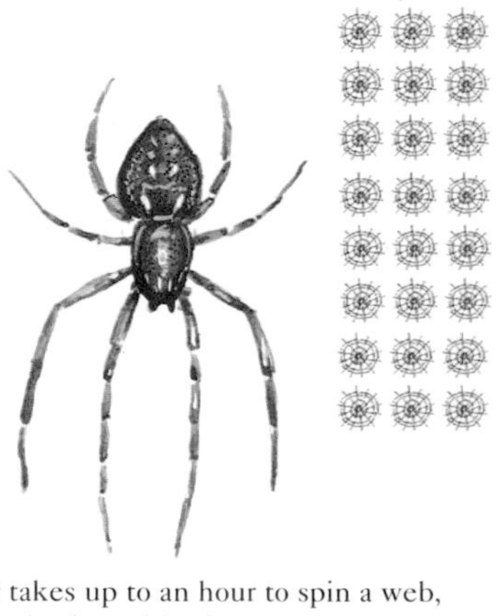

Ostrich
72 kph (45 mph). 1,728 km (1,080 miles) in one day.

Elk
72 kph (45 mph). 1,728 km (1,080 miles) in one day.

Horse
70 kph (43 mph). 1,680 km (1,032 miles) in one day.

Pheasant
59 kph (37 mph). 1,416 km (888 miles) in one day.

Harpy eagle
80 kph (50 mph), diving. 1,920 km (1,200 miles) in one day.

Pigeon
80 kph (50 mph). 1,920 km (1,200 miles) in one day.

Mallard
105 kph (65 mph). 2,520 km (1,560 miles) in one day.

Swift
Flies 1,000 km (621 miles) in one day, when foraging for insects to feed its young.

Mongolian wild ass
64 kph (40 mph). 1,536 km (960 miles) in one day.

Eider duck
76 kph (47 mph) 1,824 km (1,128 miles) in one day.

Whooper swan
88 kph (55 mph). 2,112 km (1,320 miles) in one day.

Wildebeest
80 kph (50 mph). 1,920 km (1,200 miles) in one day.

Peregrine falcon
298 kph (185 mph) when diving. 7,152 km (4,440 miles) in one day.

Lion
80 kph (50 mph). 1,920 km (1,200 miles) in one day.

Cheetah
113 kph (70 mph). 2,712 km (1,680 miles) in one day.

Thomson's gazelle
80 kph (50 mph). 1,920 km (1,200 miles) in one day.

Pronghorn antelope
98 kph (61 mph). 2,352 km (1,464 miles) in one day.

…e hunting dog
…ph (45 mph). …8 km (1,080 miles) …ne day.

Sailfish
110 kph (68 mph). 2,640 km (1,632 miles) in one day.

Flying fish
37 kph (23 mph). 888 km (552 miles) in one day.

Killer whale
56 kph (35 mph). 1,344 km (840 miles) in one day.

Bluefin tuna
74 kph (46 mph). 1,766 km (1,104 miles) in one day.

Marlin
80 kph (50 mph). 1,920 km (1,200 miles) in one day.

THE HUMAN BODY

EVERY DAY, THE HUMAN BODY needs refuelling with oxygen, food, and water. The body's powerhouse is the brain. It accounts for only two per cent of body weight, but uses 20 per cent of our oxygen intake, 20 per cent of our calorie intake, and 15 per cent of the body's blood supply. To fight disease, each body produces ten billion new white blood cells a day. Skin cells last for 25 days, red blood cells survive for 120 days, liver cells for 500 days, and some nerve cells last a whole lifetime. The continual process of cell renewal that keeps the body alive is called metabolism.

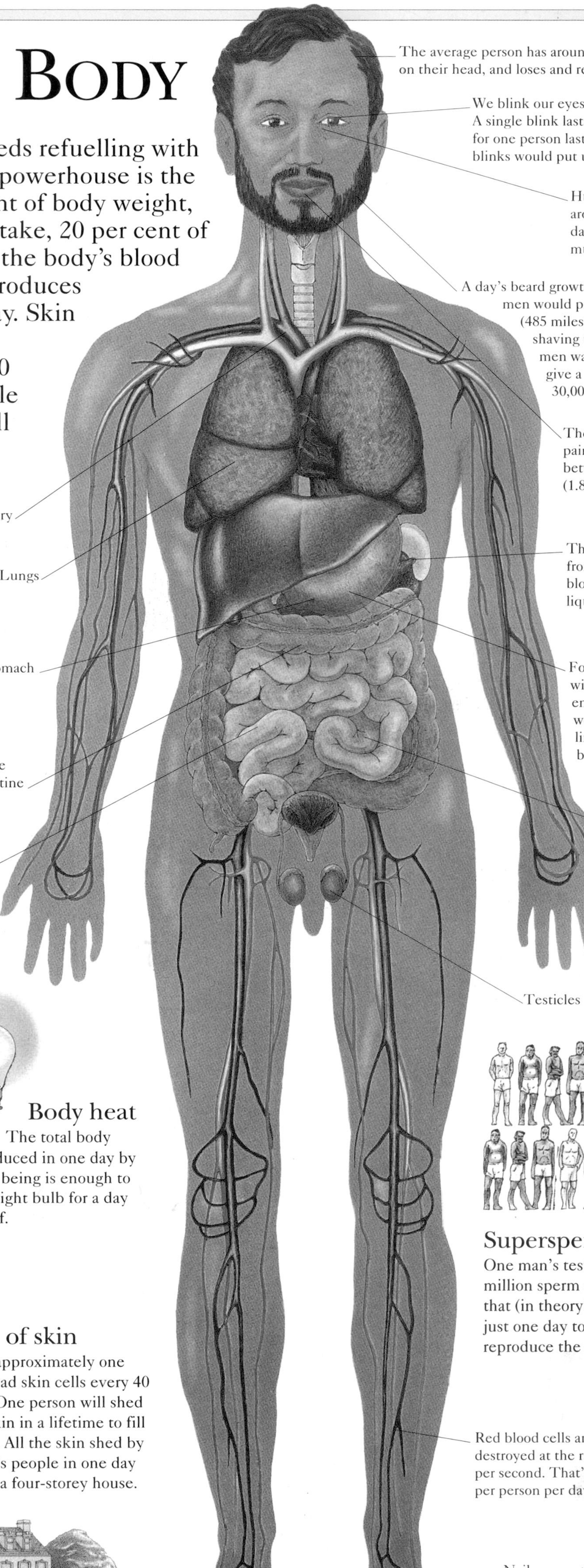

The average person has around 100,000 hairs growing on their head, and loses and replaces 100 hairs a day.

We blink our eyes on average 9,365 times every day. A single blink lasts 0.15 seconds, so a day's total blink for one person last 23 minutes. All the world's daily blinks would put us in the dark for 267,000 years.

Human tear production averages around a teaspoonful (5 ml) per day, though crying can spill that much out of the eyes in one go.

A day's beard growth for all the world's men would produce a beard 780 km (485 miles) long. If the daily shaving time of all the world's men was added up, it would give a shave that lasted 30,000 years.

The human mouth has three pairs of salivary glands, which between them produce 1 litre (1.8 pints) of saliva a day.

The kidneys filter impurities from 3,600 litres (792 gallons) of blood every day. That's enough liquid to fill 45 baths.

Food is liquidized in the stomach with the help of acids strong enough to dissolve zinc. It's no wonder that half a million cells lining the stomach die and must be replaced every minute.

It takes around 24 hours for food to travel the full length of the human digestive tract, which is 7.5 m (25 ft) long.

Red blood cells are created and destroyed at the rate of two million per second. That's 173 billion cells per person per day.

Nails grow at up to 0.1 mm (0.004 in) per day from a bed of active cells under the skin folds at their base and sides. Fingernails grow up to four times faster than toenails, and both grow faster in warm weather than in cold.

Body factory

The digestive system, lungs, and kidneys are at work around the clock. The digestive system breaks down food into particles so tiny that blood can take nourishment to all parts of the body. The body's entire blood supply passes through the lungs almost once a minute, collecting and distributing oxygen. Waste products are removed from the blood in the kidneys, each of which contains around one million tiny filters called nephrons.

Breathtaking stuff

Each one of us takes around 30,000 breaths a day. If you expelled all the air you breathed in a day into rubber dinghies, you would be able to inflate 50 two-person dinghies in 24 hours.

Bloodbath

The average human heart beats 100,800 times a day. The amount of blood that passes through the heart each day would fill 170 baths.

Body heat

The total body heat produced in one day by a human being is enough to power a light bulb for a day and a half.

House of skin

We shed approximately one million dead skin cells every 40 minutes. One person will shed enough skin in a lifetime to fill a suitcase. All the skin shed by the world's people in one day would fill a four-storey house.

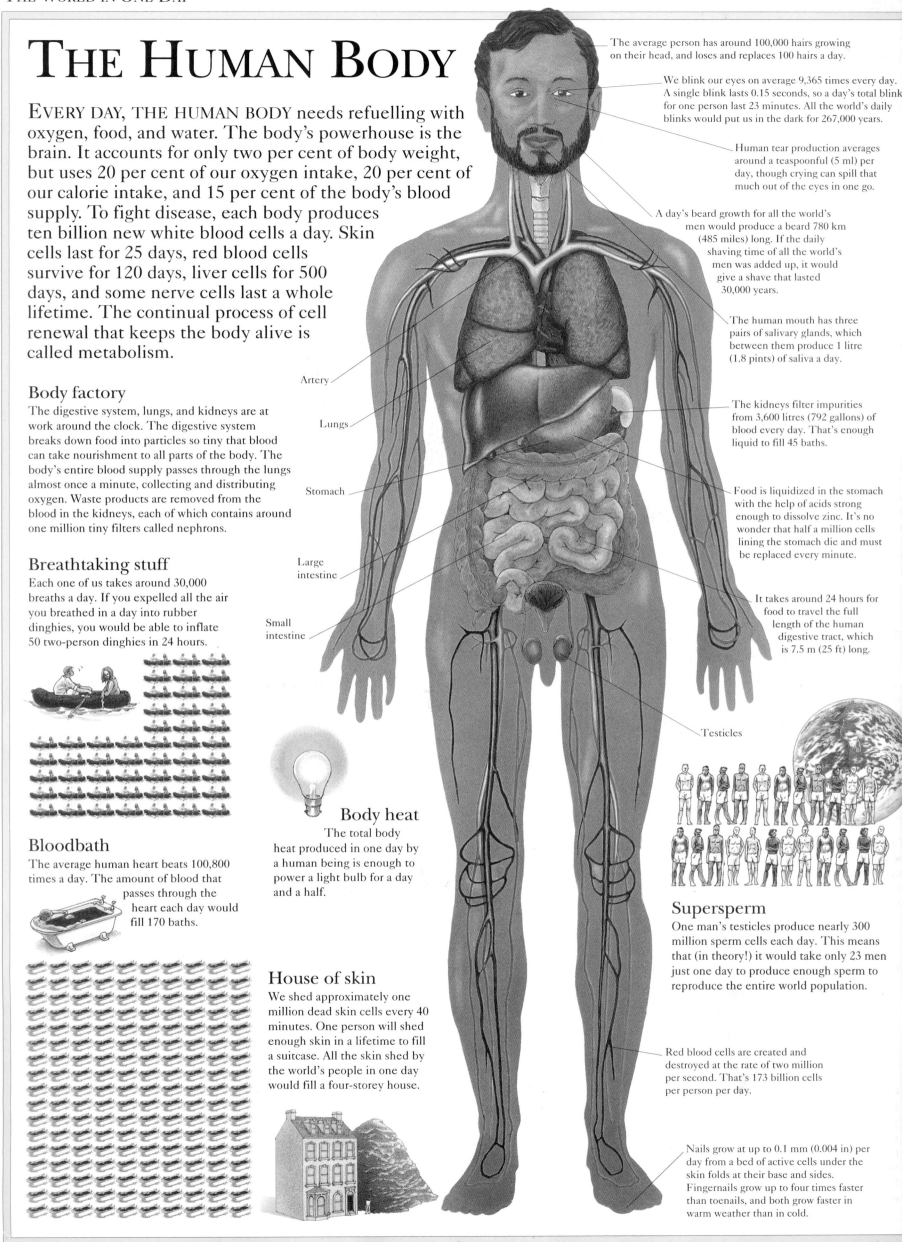

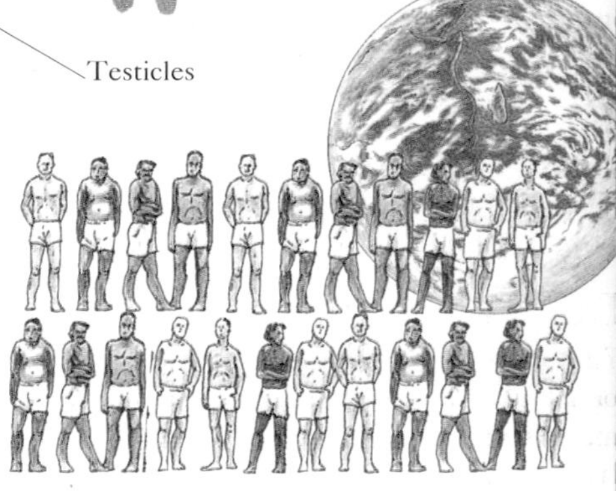

Supersperm

One man's testicles produce nearly 300 million sperm cells each day. This means that (in theory!) it would take only 23 men just one day to produce enough sperm to reproduce the entire world population.

SMALL WORLD

The human body is host to many different kinds of microorganism, including eyebrow mites and amoebas that swim on our teeth. Around ten billion bacteria live on the skin and 15 trillion bacteria live in our digestive system.

Fleas can jump 14,400 times a day in search of food, and lay up to 1,000 eggs a day.

A tick can spend a whole day feeding on human blood, and then – after it drops off the skin – a whole year without feeding again.

Tapeworms can live in the small intestine. Every day, hundreds of eggs drop off the worm and are passed in the faeces.

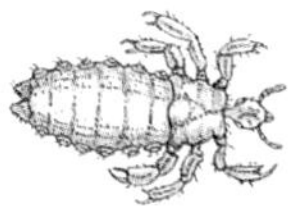

The head louse can live on the scalp. It lays up to ten eggs, called nits, every day. Head lice feed on blood that they suck through the skin.

Mother's milk

A commercial dairy cow yields 18 litres (31 pints) of milk a day. It would take 25 nursing mothers to produce as much milk in one day as a single commercial dairy cow.

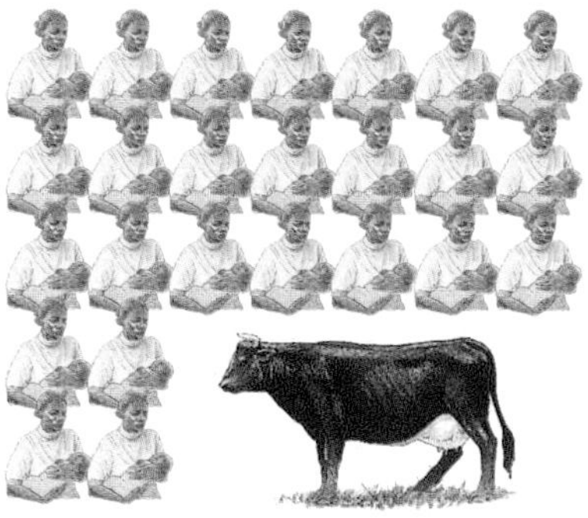

Grand flush

The body produces around 1.7 litres (3 pints) of urine a day. The total daily world production of human urine would take a full 20 minutes to pass over Niagara Falls. If everyone in the world spent five minutes a day in the only loo in the world, that loo would be engaged for 57,000 years!

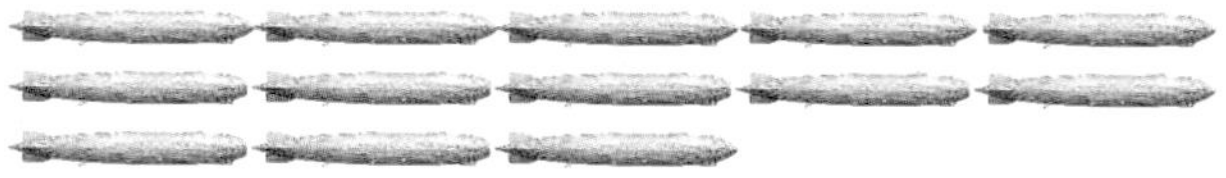

It wasn't me!

The human digestive system expels 2 litres (3.5 pints) of gas every day. The average fart is composed of 59% nitrogen, 21% hydrogen, 9% carbon dioxide, 7% methane and 4% oxygen. That means the world releases enough hydrogen in its daily farts to fill 13 Hindenburg airships.

Around 1,000 brain cells are lost per head per day. But cell losses hardly slow down the nerve impulses of the brain, which travel at around 290 kph (180 mph).

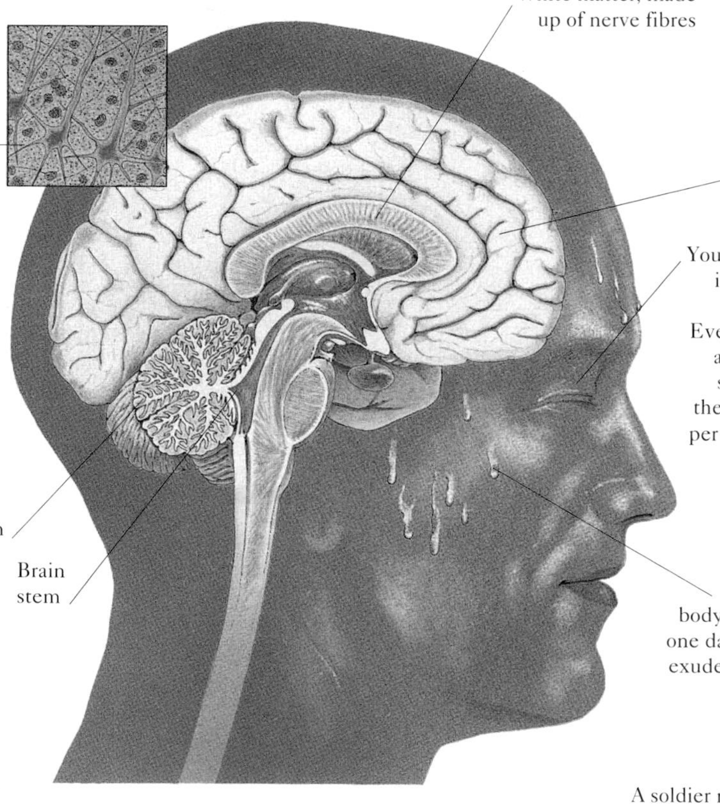

You can tell when someone is dreaming by watching their eyelids move. Everyone dreams for about a quarter of their nightly sleep, which means that the total world dream time per night is a million years!

Sweat glands are the body's cooling system. In one day the world's bodies exude enough sweat to fill 16 supertankers.

3rainy

)uring waking hours, the brain onstantly perceives and nterprets information from the enses, then initiates a response. 'he brain uses more than 100 illion neurons (nerve cells) every ay, and more than 100 trillion ynapses (nerve connections) to erform these complex functions.

ileep tight

Vhile you are awake, you are aware f what you are doing – you are onscious. When you sleep, your onscious brain switches off, but ther parts continue the vital task of eeping you alive. In a 24-hour eriod, the average person spends even hours asleep. The entire world opulation spends just over five iillion years asleep every night!

ransatlantic nails

f all the world's finger- and oenails could be joined together to nake one gigantic nail, in just one ay it would grow almost from ondon to New York.

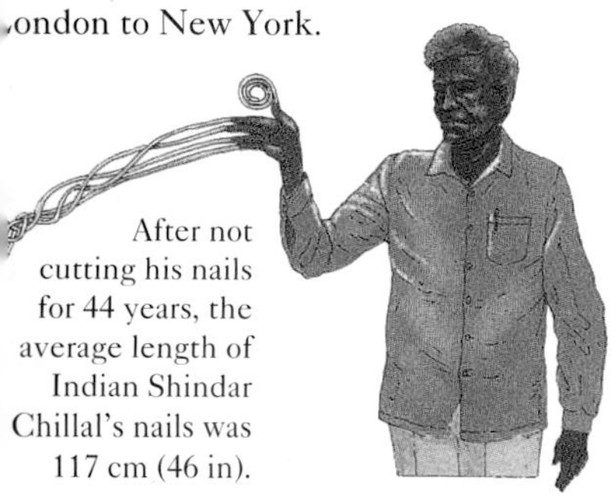

After not cutting his nails for 44 years, the average length of Indian Shindar Chillal's nails was 117 cm (46 in).

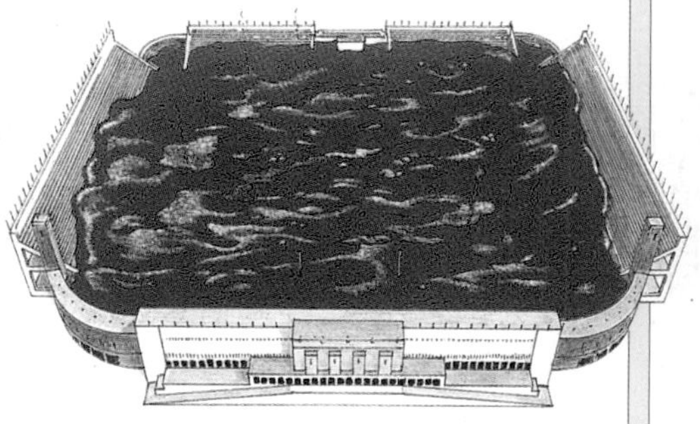

What a stink!

All the human excrement produced in one day would weigh around one million tonnes. It would fill the enormous Louisiana Superdome, New Orleans, to a depth of 19 m (62 ft).

A male office worker needs to consume 2,400 Cal (10,080 kJ) every day.

A policeman on the beat needs to eat 2,800 Cal (11,760 kJ) every day.

A soldier needs his diet to supply at least 3,500 Cal (14,700 kJ) a day.

Eating for energy

The energy given by the food we eat is measured in calories (Cal) and kilojoules (kJ). Active people need more calories each day than people who sit to work, though the body burns energy even during sleep to keep the metabolism going.

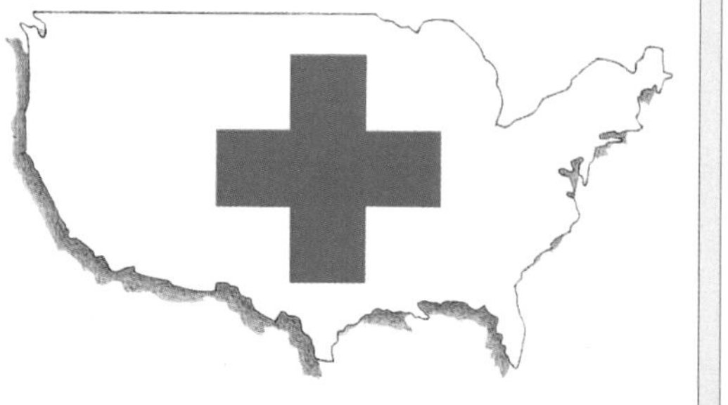

American theatre

American operating theatres are the busiest in the world. Around 64,000 operations take place in American hospitals every day. These include 1,540 hysterectomies, 960 bone grafts, 263 hernia operations, 120 cornea grafts, 27 kidney transplants, 15 skin grafts, nine liver transplants, six heart transplants, and two lung transplants.

A DAY TO REMEMBER

Discovery of X-ray

Photographic rays that pass through flesh but not through bone were discovered by William Röntgen on 8 November 1895, but not used medically until later.

First operation with anaesthetic

On 30 March 1842, Dr Crawford Long of Georgia, USA, removed a cyst from the neck of James M. Venable using ether as an anaesthetic.

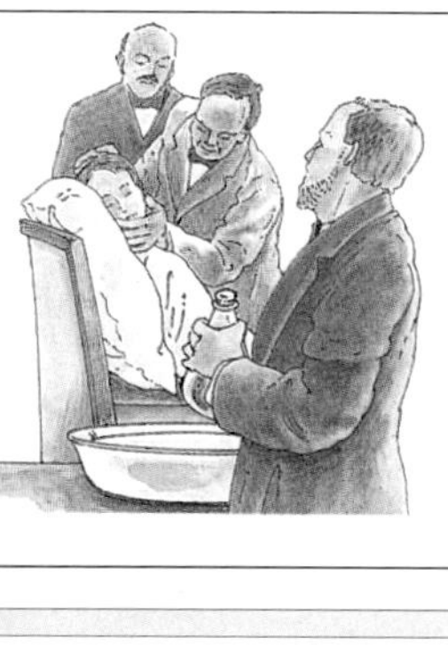

First vaccination

The first vaccination was carried out by Dr Edward Jenner, a British doctor, on 14 May 1796. Eight-year-old James Phipps was vaccinated with cowpox as protection against smallpox.

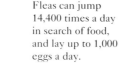

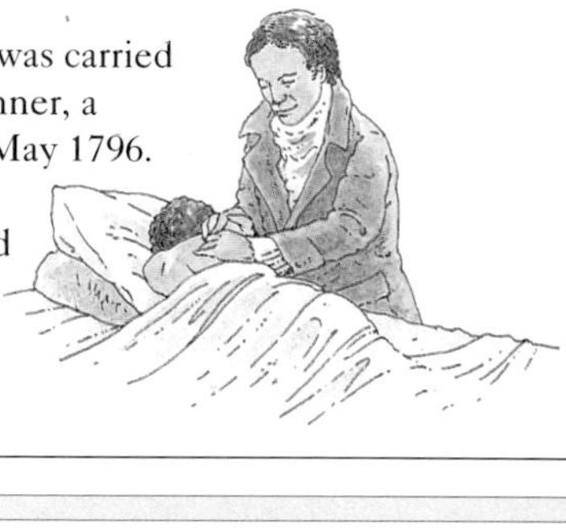

WORLD POPULATION

THE WORLD'S POPULATION IS EXPLODING FAST, with more people being born and living longer than ever before. In 1997, there were almost six billion people on Earth. The human boom is set to continue – especially in Africa, Asia, and Latin America – until, in 2080, it will peak at just over ten billion. The world's population first began to rocke about 10,000 years ago, when people began to grow their own food. The birth rate soared again in the West during the 1800s with the scientific advances of the Industrial Revolution. New methods of growing and transporting food meant that more people ate a better diet. There were also fewer deaths in childhood. Today, 12 times more people are added to the population of the world every day than 100 years ago.

India
India's current population is 952 million. 46,418 more people are added every day.

China
The population of China is 1.2 billion. 32,684 more people are added to this total every day.

Growing fast

The expanding maps along the bottom of the page show how many people are added every day to the populations of the world's 12 fastest growing countries.

Expanding cities

In many parts of the world, people are moving from rural areas to cities to find work and a better standard of living. Some of the world's largest cities are bursting at the seams, with people living in slums or shanty towns on the outskirts. Mexico City has expanded from nine million people at its heart to 24 million people. Sao Paulo has grown from nine million at the centre to 21.5 million, and Seoul from ten million to 19 million.

Mexico City
2,169 more people every day

Sao Paulo
2,090 more people every day

Seoul
1,595 more people every day

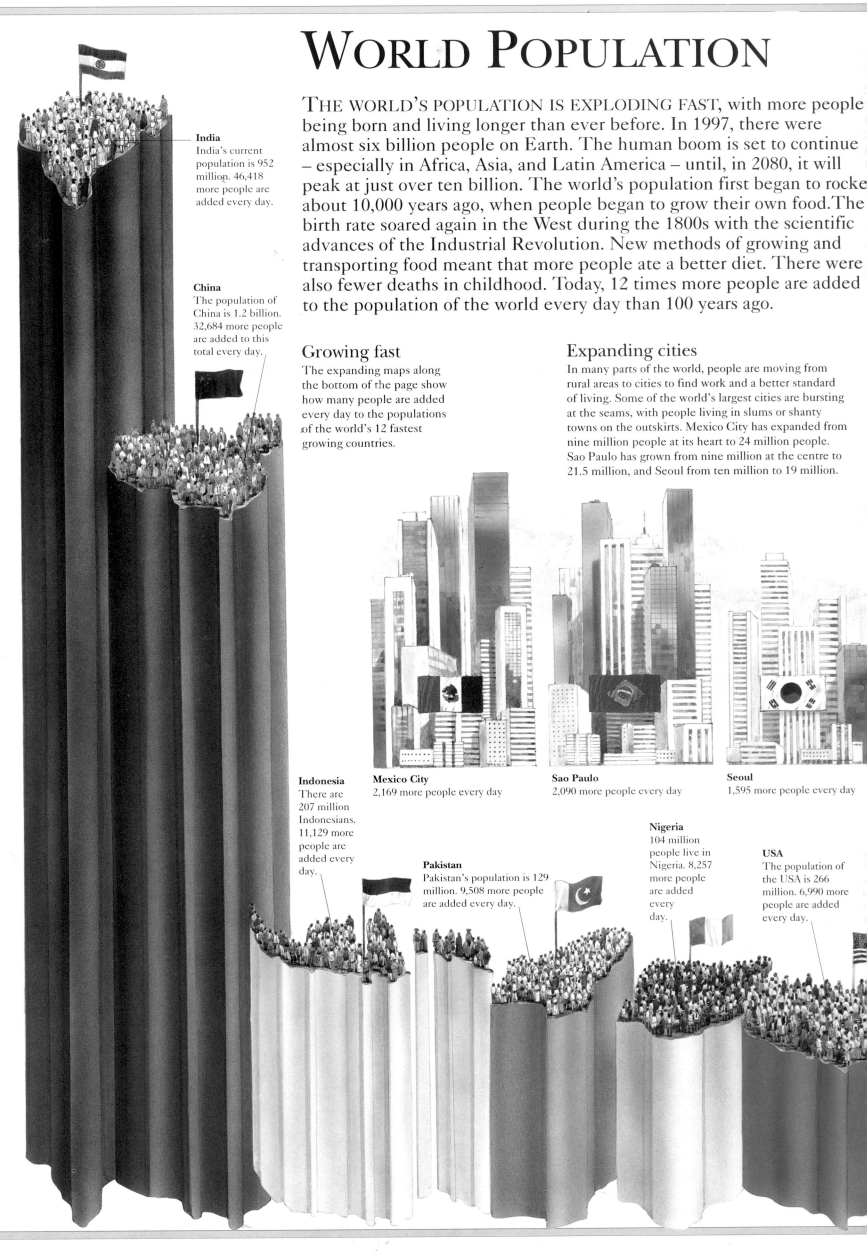

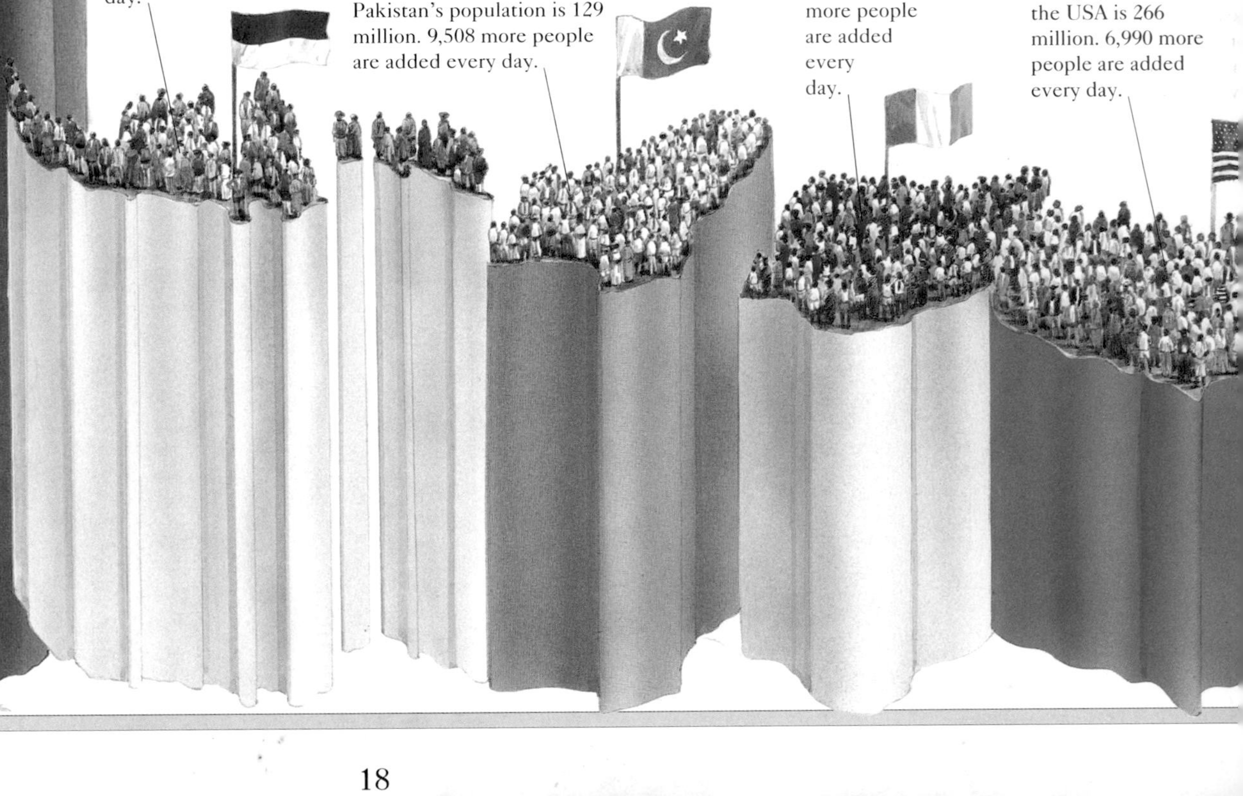

Indonesia
There are 207 million Indonesians. 11,129 more people are added every day.

Pakistan
Pakistan's population is 129 million. 9,508 more people are added every day.

Nigeria
104 million people live in Nigeria. 8,257 more people are added every day.

USA
The population of the USA is 266 million. 6,990 more people are added every day.

A DAY TO REMEMBER

Baby in a tube

The first test tube
)aby was Louise
Brown. She was born
n Oldham, in the
UK, on 25 July 1978.

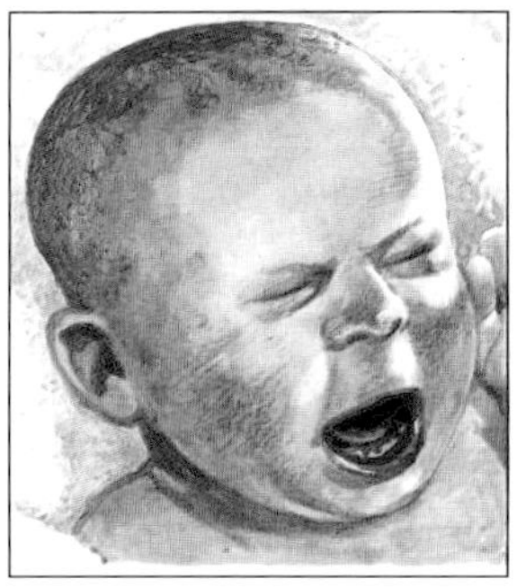

"We do!"

The largest ever wedding was conducted by Sun Myung Moon in Seoul, Korea, on 25 August 1995. He married 35,000 couples in the Olympic Stadium, and 325,000 other couples around the world by satellite link.

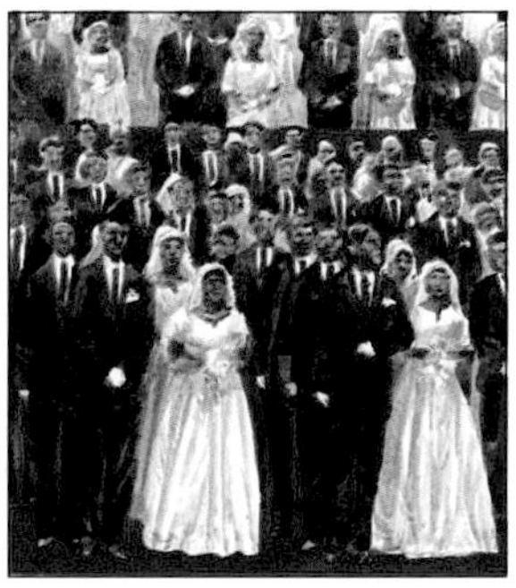

Dead cold

Dr James Bedford was the first person to be frozen after death, on 12 January 1967, in accordance with the science of cryonics. His body will be defrosted when a cure is found for the illness that killed him.

ead end

ry day around the world,
rly 150,000 people breathe
r last and die. Many die of
age, some perish in
dents or are murdered,
le fatal diseases kill
rest.

Heart disease
33,000 die every day

Diarrhoea
14,000 die every day

Cancer
13,500 die every day

Pneumonia
3,500 die every day

Tuberculosis
8,200 die every day

Malaria
5,800 die every day

Measles
4,000 die every day

Whooping cough
1,400 die every day

A whale of a day

The total weight of all the 364,321 babies born in the world in one day is 690 tonnes. This is the same weight as five blue whales.

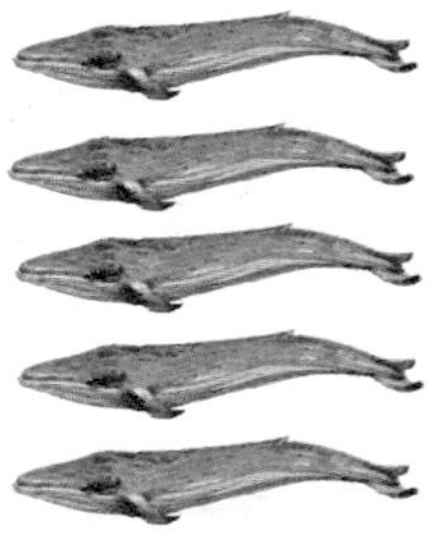

SMALL WORLD

China has more people than any other country on Earth, with a population of 1.2 billion. Overcrowding, and a shortage of resources including food, health care, and education, has caused the Chinese government to restrict family sizes in order to slow population growth rate. Chinese couples are encouraged to postpone marriage until their late 20s. In some areas, parents are allowed to have one child only.

Happy birthday!

Every day across the world, 16.5 million people celebrate their birthday. In many countries, people mark the day with a feast or party. To mark a first birthday in Korea, the child sits at a table with various objects on it – whichever he or she picks up is said to determine the child's future. Many Buddhists celebrate their birthdays by taking gifts of food to monks, and by releasing fish, turtles, and birds at the temple.

Births and deaths

n one day all over the world,
64,321 people are born and 147,137
eople die. So every day there are
17,184 more people on Earth.

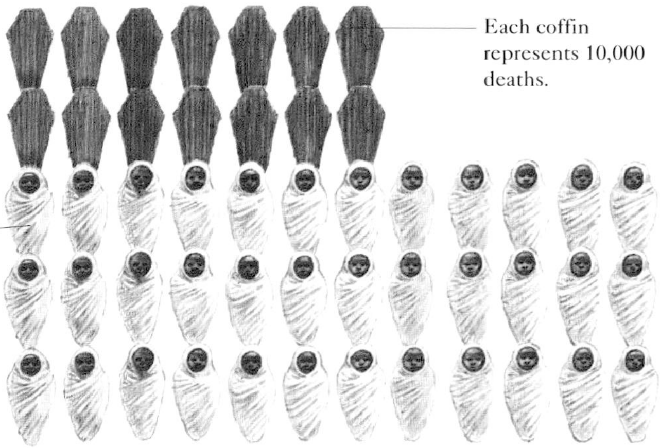

Each coffin represents 10,000 deaths.

Each baby in swaddling clothes represents 10,000 births.

Crowded planet

A hundred years from now, 378,000 people will be born every day, and 324,000 people will die. So every day, there will be 54,000 more people on Earth. In 1996, the world birth rate was 25 per 1,000, and the death rate, nine per 1,000. In 2100, the World Bank predicts that the birth rate will be down to 13 per 1,000 and the death rate up to 11 per 1,000.

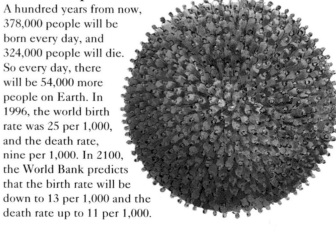

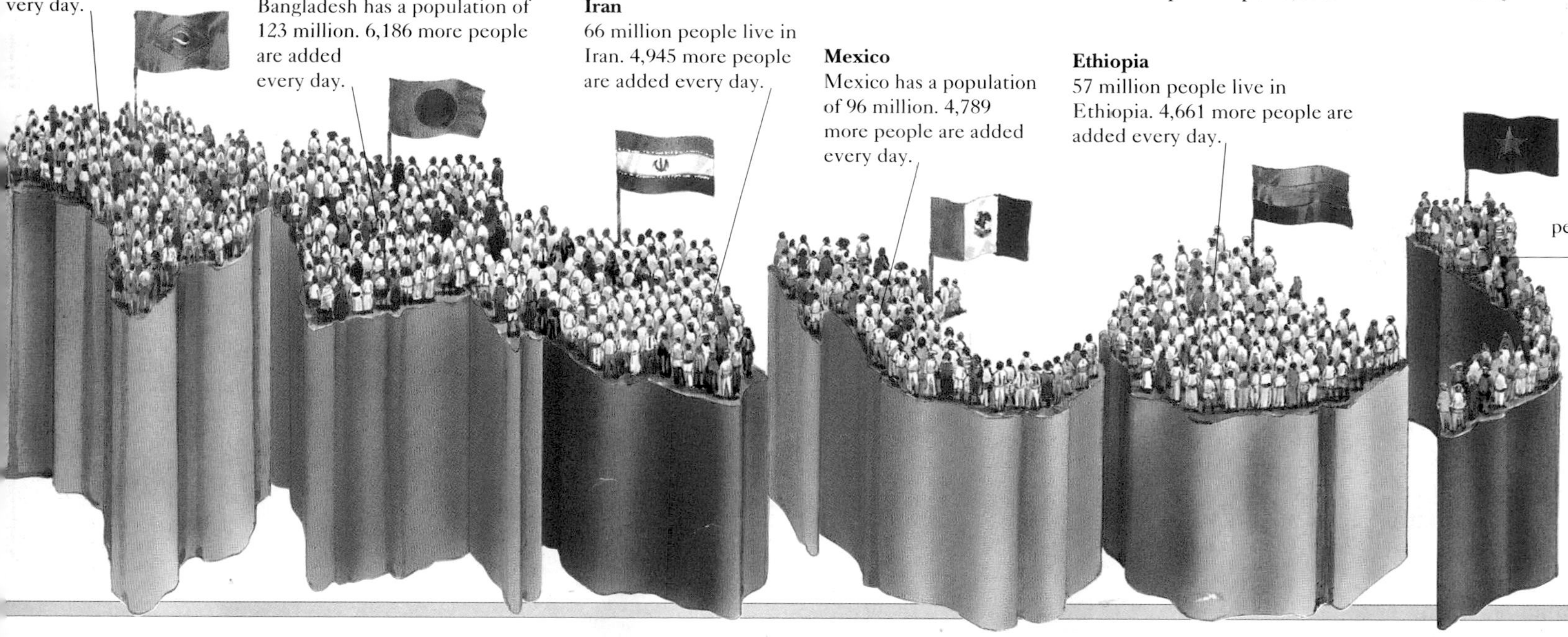

Brazil
63 million
eople live in
razil. 6,757
nore are added
very day.

Bangladesh
Bangladesh has a population of 123 million. 6,186 more people are added every day.

Iran
66 million people live in Iran. 4,945 more people are added every day.

Mexico
Mexico has a population of 96 million. 4,789 more people are added every day.

Ethiopia
57 million people live in Ethiopia. 4,661 more people are added every day.

Vietnam
Vietnam's population is 74 million. 4,315 more people are added every day.

ONE DAY'S FOOD

IT WOULD TAKE 75 SUPERTANKERS to carry one day's food for the entire planet. Most people rely on wheat, rice, and maize for their basic food. Adults need around 2,500 calories of food energy a day. However, while Westerners consume up to 4,000 calories a day, some Africans struggle on barely 1,800 calories each. And every day, 35,000 people die of starvation. Nutritious vegetables may hold the answer to the world's food needs. A field of soya beans yields 30 times as much body-building protein as a field on which beef cattle are reared.

654,000 beef cattle are slaughtered every day.

The world slaughters 2.8 million pigs a day.

1.2 million sheep are slaughtered every day.

Almost 70 million chickens are slaughtered every day worldwide.

Meat

Every day, the world eats 533,000 tonnes of meat, the same weight as a herd of a million cows. But if everyone had a share of the world's meat, there would be barely enough for two mouthfuls a day each.

Food city

This is what the world's daily helpings of some of its most nutritious foodstuffs would look like, delivered into the heart of a modern city.

Potatoes
We dig up 727,000 tonnes of potatoes every day.

Beans and lentils
In one day, the world produces 161,000 tonnes of beans and lentils.

Grapes
The world's grape harvest for one day weighs 155,000 tonnes – that's 22 billion individual grapes.

Bananas
The world's daily banana harvest is 144,000 tonnes.

Cabbages
The world produces 110,000 tonnes of cabbages in a day.

Watermelons
Every day 80,000 tonnes of watermelons are harvested.

Cocoa
The world produces 7,000 tonnes of cocoa beans every day. That's enough to make 600 million bars of chocolate.

Peas
Every day, the world harvests 12,000 tonnes of peas. That's enough to serve 300 million people with a portion of peas.

Tea
Worldwide 7,000 tonnes of tea leaves are produced every day. That's enough for three billion cups of tea.

Cucumbers
The world grows 53,000 tonnes of cucumbers every day. That's enough for everyone in India and China to have a cucumber sandwich each.

Onions
The world's daily onion harvest weighs 89,000 tonnes, as much as the ocean liner *Queen Elizabeth*.

Salt
The world harvest 500,000 tonnes of salt in a day.

The fastest food in the world

Every day, Americans get through seven million pizzas, 4,000 tonnes of potato crisps, 400 tonnes of pretzels, 300,000 tins of Spam, around 15 million burgers, 15 million litres (26 million pints) of ice cream, 250 million Coca-Colas, as well as five chips each.

Eggs

Eggs are a complete food because they provide all the proteins the body needs for tissue growth and repair. Today, China is the world's biggest egg-producing nation. The world's hen population lays nearly two billion eggs a day. They would make an omelette as big as the island of Cyprus.

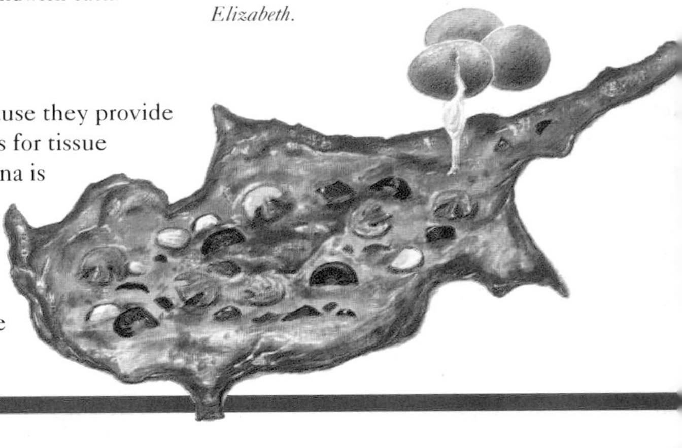

Japan

The Japanese eat 25,000 tonnes of fish a day.

France

The French love the pungent flavour of garlic. France produces 145 tonnes of garlic every day.

China

The Chinese lead the world in rice production. They eat rice at every meal, getting through 365,000 tonnes every day.

Greece

The Greeks eat more bread than anyone else in the world – 300 g (9 oz) per person per day.

Wheat
Wheat is one of the world's major food crops, with 1.4 million tonnes harvested every day. The world's daily portion of wheat weighs the same as 3,757 fully laden jumbo jets.

Rice
Nearly 1.5 million tonnes of rice are harvested every day and about half of the world's population eat it as the main part of their meals. The world's daily helping of rice would make a heap six times as big as Egypt's Great Pyramid.

Tomatoes
All the tomatoes eaten in the world in one day weigh 212,000 tonnes.

Maize
Every day 1.6 million tonnes of maize are harvested, and the world eats a portion of maize that weighs as much as 300,000 African elephants.

Oranges
The orange is probably the world's most popular fruit – 160,000 tonnes are picked every day.

Pineapples
The world produces 32,000 tonnes of pineapples every day.

Sugar
The world produces 134,000 tonnes of sugar a day.

Apples
The world's daily apple harvest is 134,000 tonnes.

Lemons and limes
In one day, the world produces 21,000 tonnes of lemons and limes.

Apricots
The world's daily apricot harvest weighs 6,000 tonnes and would fill six barges.

Garlic
Worldwide, 22,000 tonnes of garlic are produced every day.

Avocados
The world avocado harvest weighs in at 5,000 tonnes a day.

Pumpkins
The world produces 23,000 tonnes of pumpkins in a day.

Mangos
In one day the world produces 51,000 tonnes of mangos.

Strawberries
The world's daily consumption of strawberries is 6,000 tonnes.

Raspberries
The world produces enough raspberries every day to fill a train pulling 23 trucks.

Carrots
The world produces 39,000 tonnes of carrots every day.

Coconuts
In one day the world produces 121,000 tonnes of coconuts.

Caviare
The world produces 2.7 tonnes of caviare in a day.

High-flying food

Nearly three million meals are served in the air every day.

Honey

In one day, bees sip the nectar from three trillion flowers. They make 3,000 tonnes of honey, enough to spread a slice of toast as big as London.

OUT OF THIS WORLD

The first astronauts ate cold paste which they squeezed from a tube. Today's astronauts have a menu of more than 70 items. Some of these are in cans or foil bags. Others need water to be added. Many are heated before eating. Astronauts eat from trays strapped to their laps.

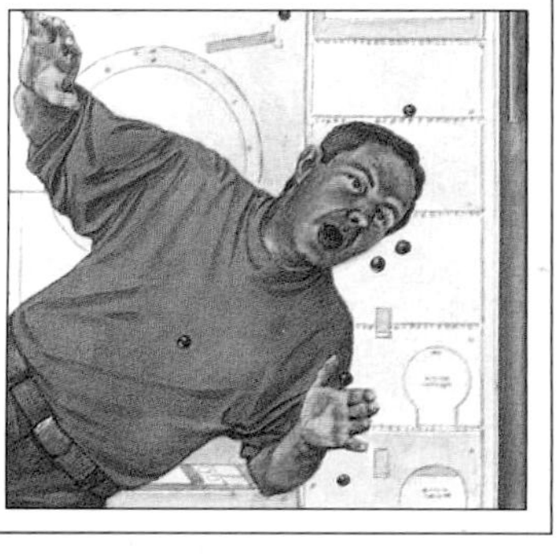

PRODUCTION

THE WORLD IS A mighty production machine; every day its factories and offices churn out more than £50 billion worth of stuff. It's strange to think that machines were invented less than 300 years ago, and before that time, everything was made at home, by hand. The first machines were powered by renewable energy – the sweat of human effort, and water turning a wheel. But the age of steam was fired by coal, so the first really efficient machines began to gobble up the Earth's natural resources. Today, the world uses the equivalent of 4 kg (8 lb) of oil per person a day – though Americans consume five and a half times that amount!

What a gas!

Every day, world natural gas production is nearly 6 billion cu m (212 billion cu ft). One day's gas for the whole world would fill 2.6 million hot-air balloons.

Coal

The world produces 12 million tonnes of coal a day. This gives a daily heap of coal as tall as the Eiffel Tower.

Hoover Dam

Cement

The world produces 3.2 million tonnes of cement in a day. This would make 16 million tonnes of concrete – enough to build three Hoover Dams.

Jewel in the crown

274,000 carats of diamonds are mined every day. A carat is 0.02 g, so the world's daily output of diamonds is less than 5.5 kg (12 lb).

Dam powerful

The world's hydroelectric dams produce 2.4 billion kWh of electricity every day. So, each day, they save the world from burning 600,000 tonnes of oil. One day's hydroelectricity for the world could power a 100W lightbulb for a billion days – 2.7 million years.

Black gold

The world produces almost nine million tonnes of oil a day, which is enough to fill the holds of 90 supertankers. Every day in the world's refineries, 2.3 million tonnes of oil is turned into petrol, and 1.4 million tonnes is used to manufacture plastics.

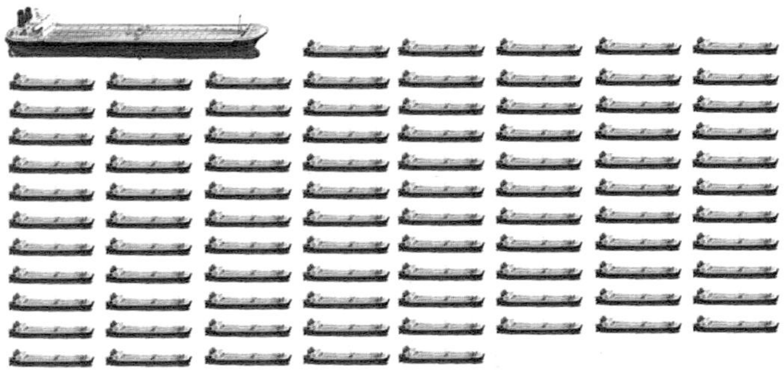

Crude wealth

A typical oil rig can pump up 189,000 barrels of precious crude oil from the Earth every day.

Neon city

A nuclear power station could produce enough electricity in a day to supply the city of Las Vegas for eight years.

Cars, cars cars

Every day, a staggering 137,000 vehicles roll off the world's production lines. The USA is the world's biggest car manufacturer, but the people of Luxembourg own more cars per head than any other nation in the world. In Luxembourg, there are 57 cars on the road for every 100 people.

USA
The USA produces 32,836 vehicles a day.

Japan
Japan manufactures 27,933 vehicles every day.

France
The French manufacture 9,520 vehicles daily.

Germany
12,787 vehicles roll off Germany's production lines each day.

South Korea
In South Korea, 6,922 vehicles are produced every day.

Canada
Every day Canada's factories produce over 6,662 vehicles.

Spain
Spain manufactures 6,394 vehicles a day.

UK
4,836 vehicles roll out of the assembly plant every day in the UK.

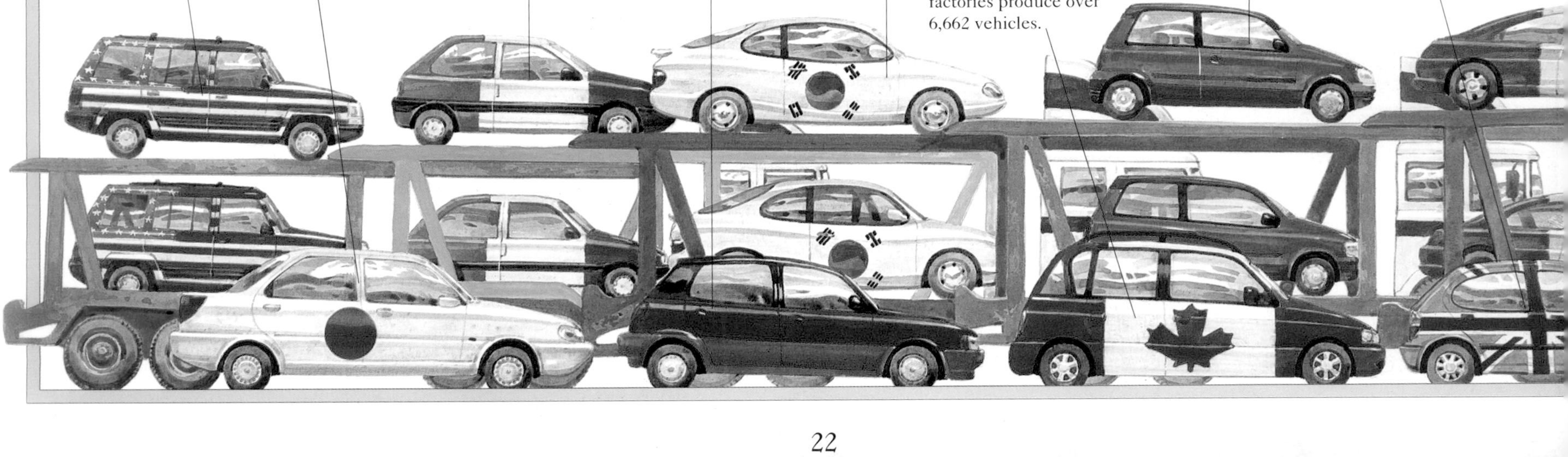

Money World

The world's banks send money to each other 24 hours a day. Instead of cash, they transmit computer messages giving the amount. In one day, banks exchange over 1.5 million electronic messages. In this way, about £2 trillion moves around the globe every day. As well as money itself, the global financial markets trade in stocks and bonds, which may be shares in business companies. The total value of the world's tradeable stocks and bonds is £8.5 trillion.

Awesome ores

Metals are extracted from ores, naturally occurring minerals that are mined from the Earth.

The world produces 30,000 tonnes of copper every day. That would make enough copper piping to encircle the globe three times.

555,000 tonnes of aluminium are produced in a day, enough to make more than 17 billion coke cans.

The world's mines yield 100 tonnes of uranium every day. Uranium is used to power nuclear reactors.

Daily world production of platinum is 80 kg (176 lb). It is used in electrical instruments and jewellery.

The world output of mercury is eight tonnes a day, enough to fill nearly seven million thermometers.

Gold rush

6.3 tonnes of gold is mined in one day – more than a quarter of it comes from South Africa. Gold is so dense that the world's daily gold extraction could fit inside a fridge. Every day, 150 kg (330 lb) of gold (much of it recycled) is used to fill teeth – that's the weight of more than 2 adults.

A new car every day

The number of cars in the world is increasing at a little more than half the rate of world population growth. Every day, at least one new car is produced for every other additional person on the planet.

Great heaps of stuff

If all the tonnes of different stuff produced in the world in a single day could be piled up into heaps, the landscape would be dominated by mountains of useful goods. The daily soap powder heap would be big enough to ski down, and one day's timber pile would reach right up into outer space.

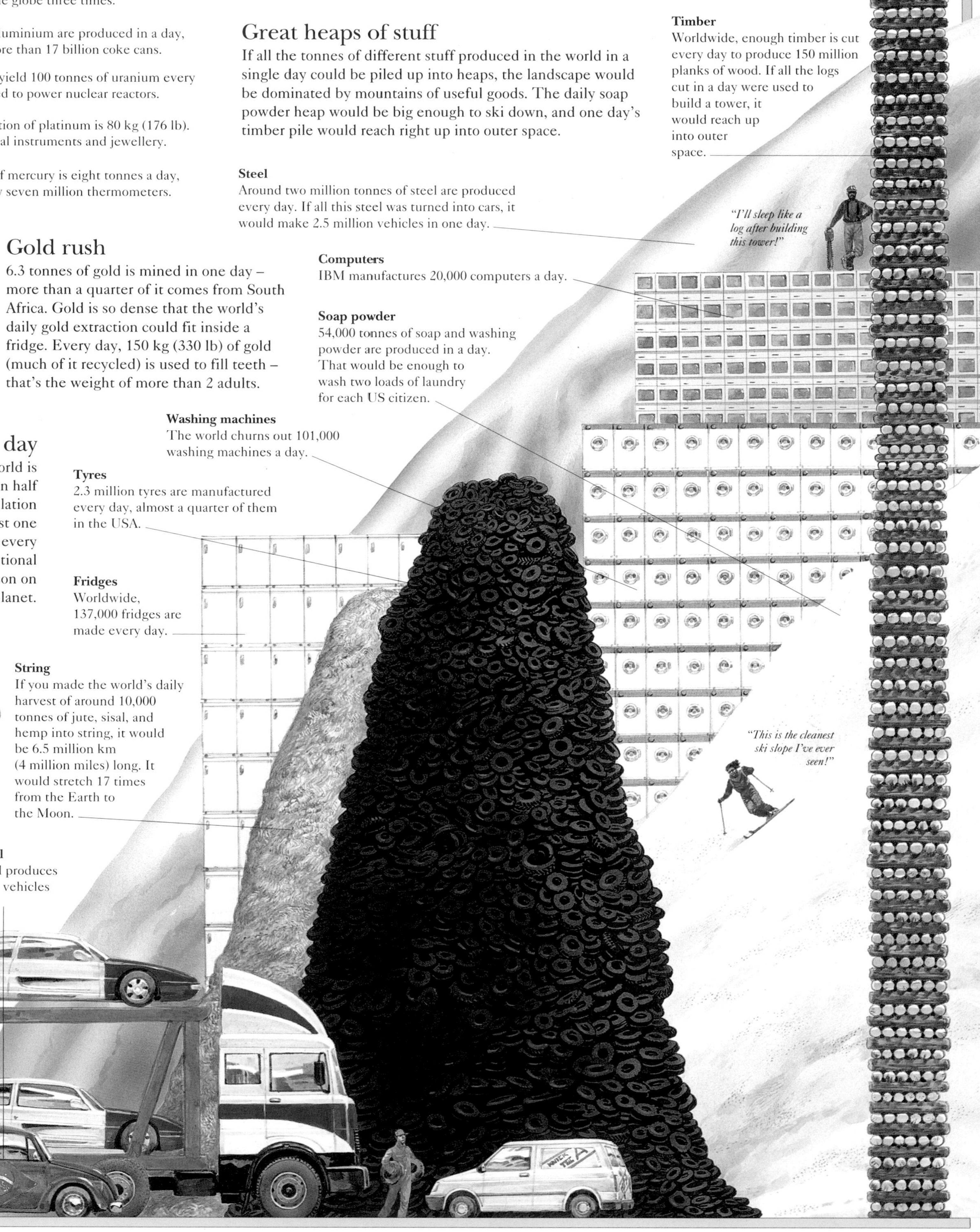
"This pile of timber was built in one day, and it reaches right up into space – or so they tell me!"
"I'll sleep like a log after building this tower!"
"This is the cleanest ski slope I've ever seen!"

Timber
Worldwide, enough timber is cut every day to produce 150 million planks of wood. If all the logs cut in a day were used to build a tower, it would reach up into outer space.

Steel
Around two million tonnes of steel are produced every day. If all this steel was turned into cars, it would make 2.5 million vehicles in one day.

Computers
IBM manufactures 20,000 computers a day.

Soap powder
54,000 tonnes of soap and washing powder are produced in a day. That would be enough to wash two loads of laundry for each US citizen.

Washing machines
The world churns out 101,000 washing machines a day.

Tyres
2.3 million tyres are manufactured every day, almost a quarter of them in the USA.

Fridges
Worldwide, 137,000 fridges are made every day.

String
If you made the world's daily harvest of around 10,000 tonnes of jute, sisal, and hemp into string, it would be 6.5 million km (4 million miles) long. It would stretch 17 times from the Earth to the Moon.

Italy
4,568 vehicles are manufactured in Italy every day.

Brazil
Brazil produces 3,737 vehicles daily.

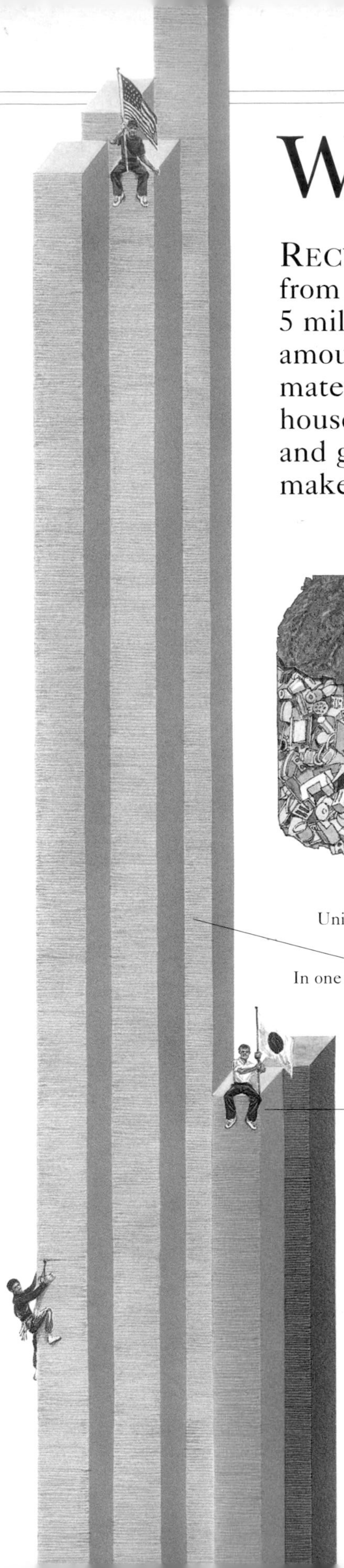

WASTE AND RECYCLING

RECYCLING RUBBISH MEANS that we take fewer raw materials from the Earth. Recycling paper the world over saves cutting down 5 million trees every day. Recycling also helps to save energy. The amount of energy needed to make one aluminium can from raw materials will make 20 cans from recycled aluminium. Most household waste can be recycled. Kitchen scraps can be composted, and glass taken to a bottle bank to be crushed and melted down to make new glass. Plastics can be shredded, melted, and reformed.

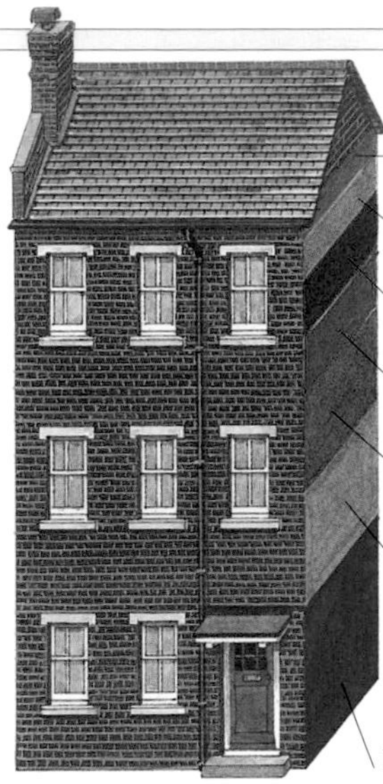

Wasteful house

In one day, the average British household generates 1.74 kg (4 lb) of rubbish bin waste. In a year, this grows to the equivalent of the weight of 11 adults.

Nappy mountain

Babies in the USA get through 7,500 tonnes of disposable nappies every day. A day's worth of soiled nappies would fill 100,000 dustbins. Piled up, they would make a mountain as big as a 10-storey building.

Loads of rubbish

The world's top ten rubbish producers range from the USA with 2 kg (4 lb) of waste per person per day, to Japan, with 1 kg (2 lb).

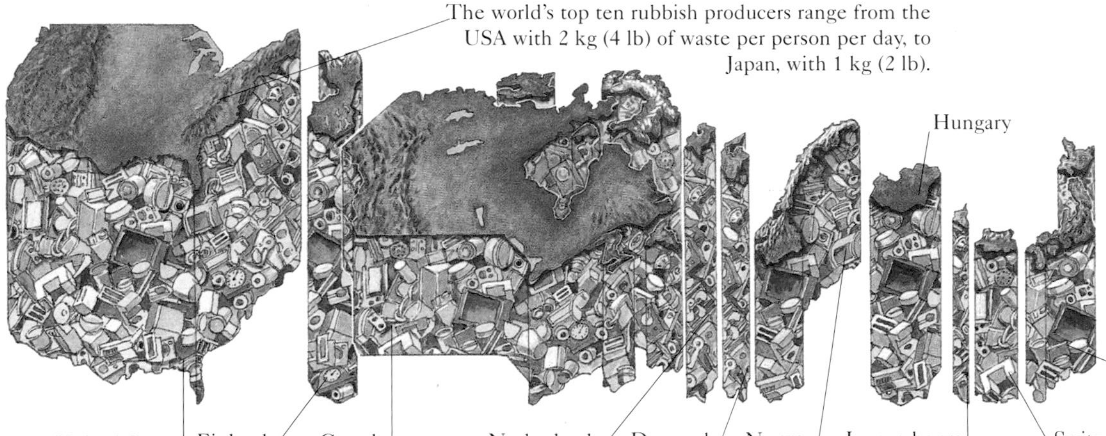

World rubbish

If everyone in the world produced garbage at the rate of the average American, the world rubbish dump would grow by 12 million tonnes a day – equivalent to the weight of a herd of 2.4 million elephants. Fortunately, the world's rubbish heap grows by a mere two million tonnes every day.

Deforestation

Every day, enough tropical rainforest is cut down to cover an island as big as Barbados. During the 1980s, an area of forest was cut down that would have completely covered Germany.

One 12-m (40-ft) tree will make a stack of newspapers 1.2 m (4 ft) high.

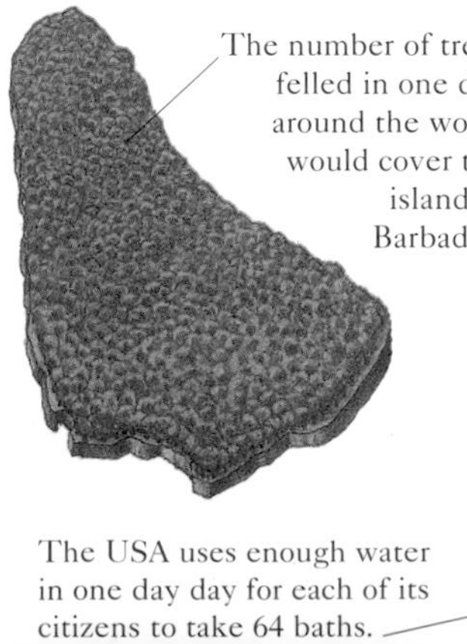

The number of trees felled in one day around the world would cover the island of Barbados.

Paper in the USA

In one day, the USA throws away 202,000 tonnes of paper, of which 70,000 tonnes is recycled.

Paper in Japan

Japan uses 70,000 tonnes of paper in one day, and recycles more than half of it.

Piles of waste

The large illustration shows waste and recycling figures for paper, cars, newspaper, kitchen appliances, tyres, cans, and clothes. The USA and Japan lag behind Germany, which has strict laws about recycling. It recycles around 20,000 tonnes of packaging materials in one day.

Cars

In the USA, 32,000 tonnes of cars are put on the scrap heap every day. 24,000 tonnes of materials from them are recycled.

Newspapers

28,000 tonnes of newsprint is dumped every day in the USA, of which 13,000 tonnes is recycled. Each Sunday edition of the *New York Times* produces 3,600 tonnes of waste.

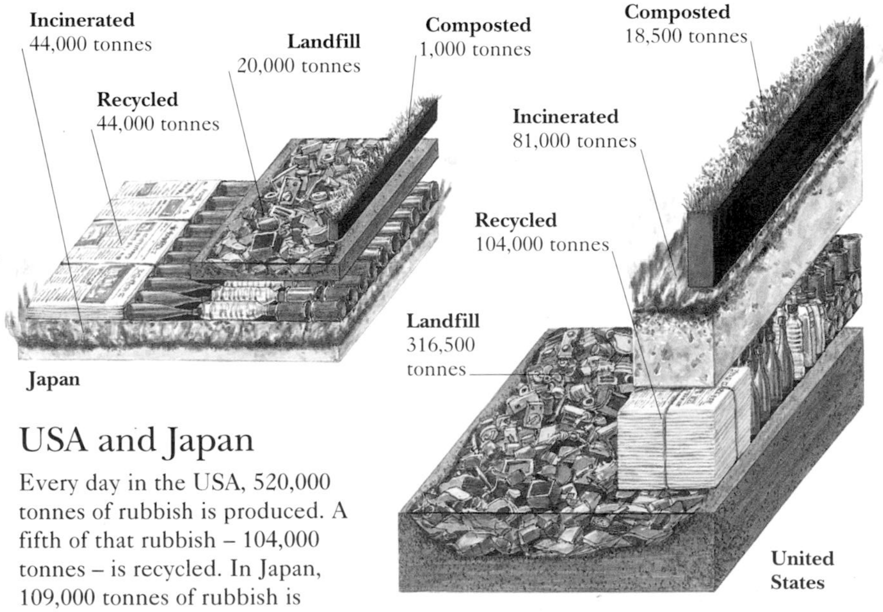

USA and Japan

Every day in the USA, 520,000 tonnes of rubbish is produced. A fifth of that rubbish – 104,000 tonnes – is recycled. In Japan, 109,000 tonnes of rubbish is produced in one day. Japan recycles almost half its rubbish – 44,000 tonnes every day. Yet both countries are still very wasteful. Japan dumps 82,000 disposable plastic cameras every day. In the USA, 19,000 cu m (685,000 cu ft) of loose plastic "peanuts" are used in packaging every day – that's enough to fill 43 American homes or the passenger compartments of 22 jumbo jets.

The USA uses enough water in one day day for each of its citizens to take 64 baths.

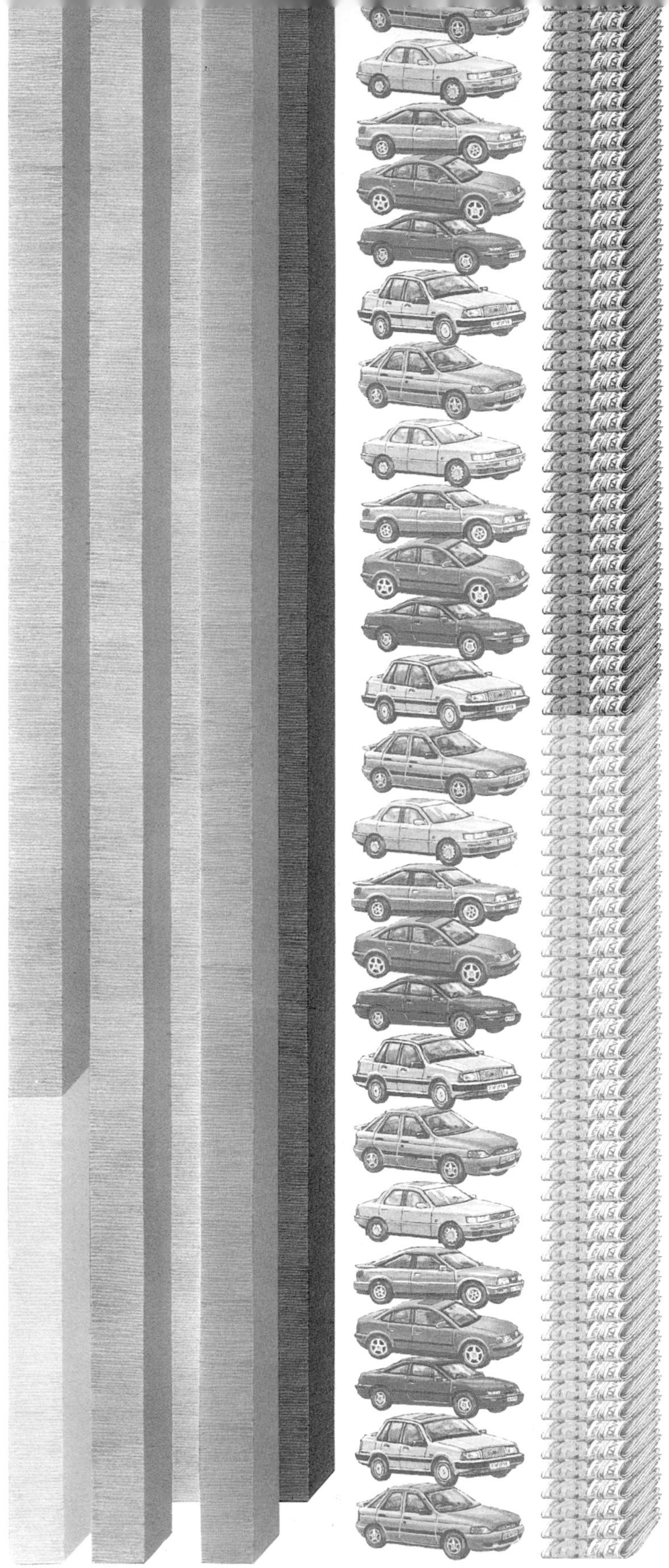

Released into the atmosphere 69 %

Dumped into surface water 3 %

Deposited on land 13 %

Buried underground 15 %

Dumping ground
This cross section shows where toxic waste is dumped.

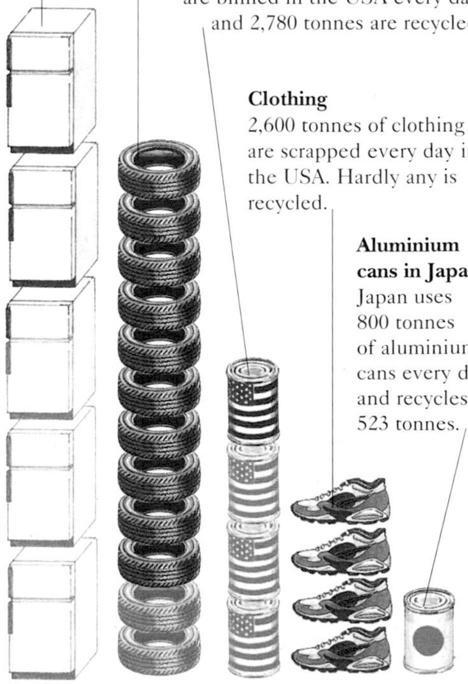

Kitchen appliances
In one day, the USA dumps 8,400 tonnes of large kitchen appliances. 4,700 tonnes of materials from them are recycled.

Rubber tyres
7,400 tonnes of tyres are dumped every day in the USA. More than 1,000 tonnes of them are recycled.

Aluminium cans
4,250 tonnes of aluminium cans are binned in the USA every day, and 2,780 tonnes are recycled.

Clothing
2,600 tonnes of clothing are scrapped every day in the USA. Hardly any is recycled.

Aluminium cans in Japan
Japan uses 800 tonnes of aluminium cans every day, and recycles 523 tonnes.

Toxic waste

Vegetation in many areas of the USA has been damaged by acid rain. This is because the USA releases almost 3,000 tonnes of toxic chemicals into the atmosphere in one day. That's a whole load of poisonous chemicals weighing as much as 15 Statues of Liberty every single day.

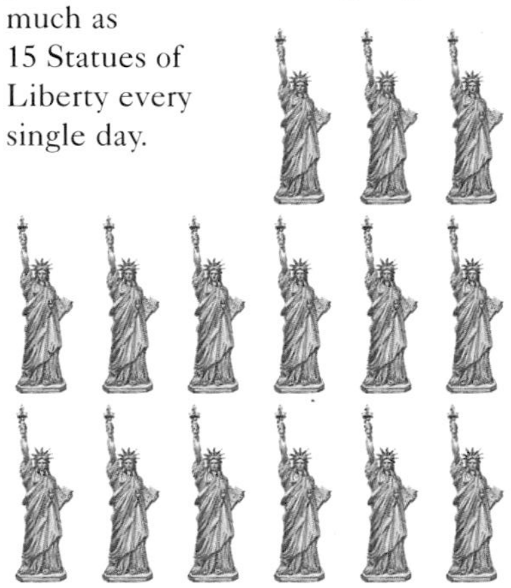

Oil spillage

The amount of oil spilled in the sea and on land in one day would fill up five Olympic-sized swimming pools.

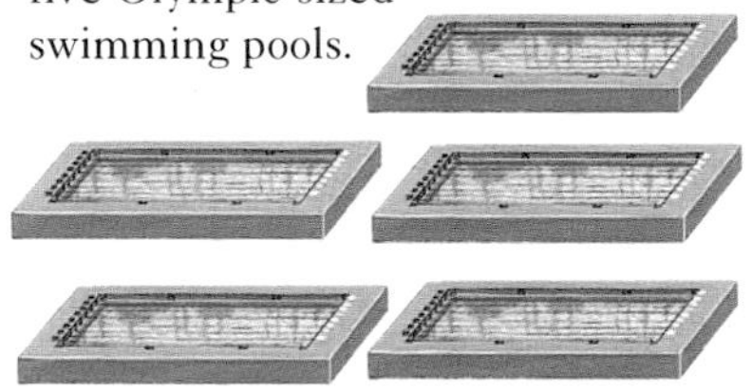

Steel cans

13 million steel cans are recycled every day in the USA. That's 9,000 steel cans every minute of the day, or 150 a second!

12:00
12:01

Cans have wings

All the aluminium cans binned in one day in the USA would build 16 DC-10 airliners.

"Sacré bleu! That's not on my navigation chart!"

Sea dumping

Every day, 18,000 tonnes of litter is chucked into the world's seas – the same weight as two Eiffel Towers or 136 blue whales. That rubbish includes 450,000 non-biodegradable plastic containers.

Bath in the loo

In the Western world, everyone uses around 135 litres (30 gallons) of water every day just to flush the loo. That's enough for one and a half baths.

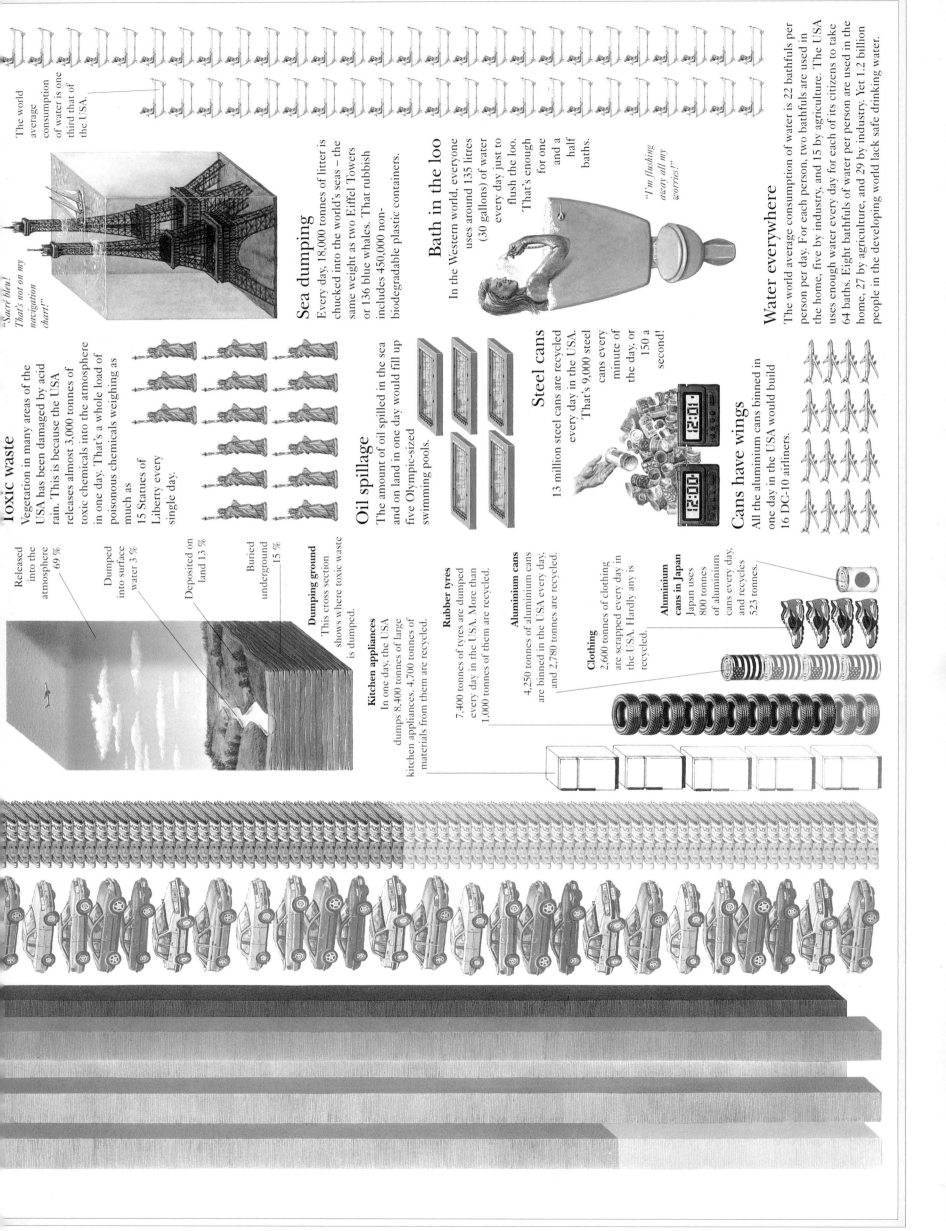

"I'm flushing away all my worries!"

The world average consumption of water is one third that of the USA.

Water everywhere

The world average consumption of water is 22 bathfuls per person per day. For each person, two bathfuls are used in the home, five by industry, and 15 by agriculture. The USA uses enough water every day for each of its citizens to take 64 baths. Eight bathfuls of water per person are used in the home, 27 by agriculture, and 29 by industry. Yet 1.2 billion people in the developing world lack safe drinking water.

COMMUNICATIONS

WORDS WERE FIRST SPOKEN BY HUMAN MOUTHS into human ears around 40,000 years ago. Today, words can reach destinations on the other side of the globe almost as soon as they are uttered. Radio signals are bounced back to receiving stations by the Earth's atmosphere, and satellites in space allow people to talk to each other, face to face, day and night, right across the planet. Our voices have escaped into space in the form of radio waves, and our first words have passed within 70 light years of the Sun. We have also beamed out messages, hoping to get in touch with alien beings – but as yet, no signal has been received from other worlds.

How satellite communications work

High-frequency signals for telephone, computer, and television pass straight through Earth's atmosphere. They need satellites in space to bounce them back to Earth. The higher the satellite, the greater the area of Earth it can cover.

UOSAT 12
Each day, University of Surrey Satellite 12 travels 16 times around the Earth. It is testing a propulsion system that uses steam instead of poisonous gas.

OPTUS B
Optus B travels 864,000 k (540,000 miles) each day, providing Australia and the Pacific with telephone and broadcasting links.

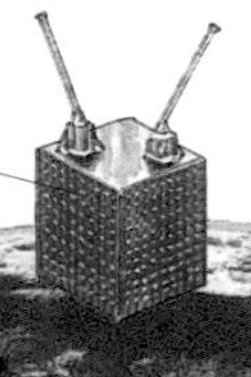

Defense Support Program
DSP is a US missile-warning satellite. Its infrared sensors can detect hot exhaust from a nuclear missile. It scans the surface of the Earth at six revolutions per minute, which is 8,640 times a day.

SOHO
Every day, SOHO (Solar and Heliospheric Observatory) measures millions of sunquakes or vibrations on the surface of the Sun.

Iridium
This is one of a series of 66 low-Earth orbit communications satellites launched in 1997. Each day, Iridium can transfer thousands of calls from mobile phones.

Infrared Space Observatory
Each day, the tank of supercold helium in ISO cools instruments to –271° C, and allows them to measure tiny amounts of heat arriving from planets, gas clouds, and galaxies.

Molniya
Molniya provides communications coverage (television and telephone calls) for the most northerly regions of Russia for about eight hours every day.

Space Shuttle
In one day, the Space Shuttle can carry a crew of seven astronauts around the world 16 times, while they service and repair other craft, carry out scientific experiments, or take hundreds of photos of Earth.

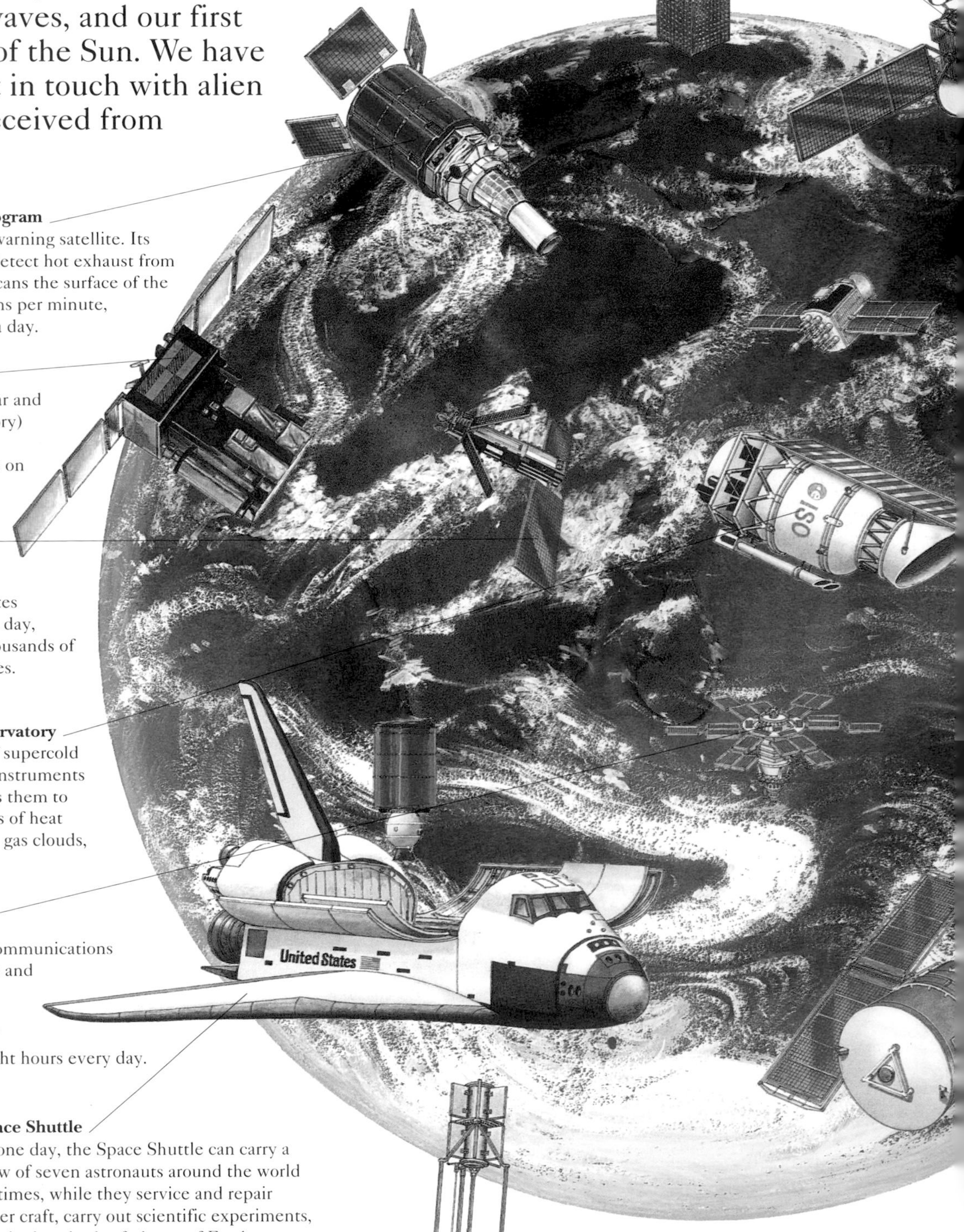

Meteosat weather satellite

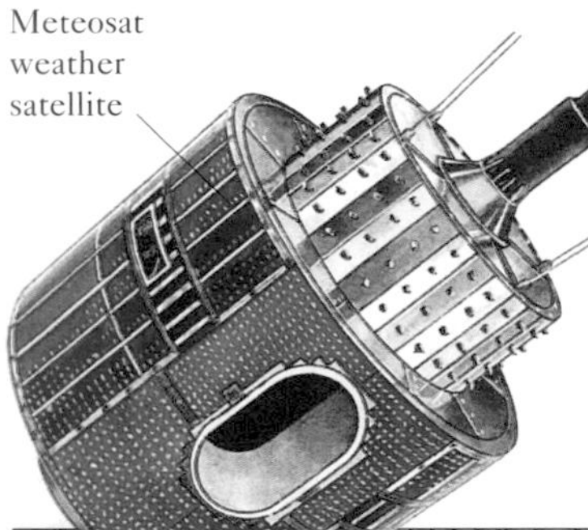

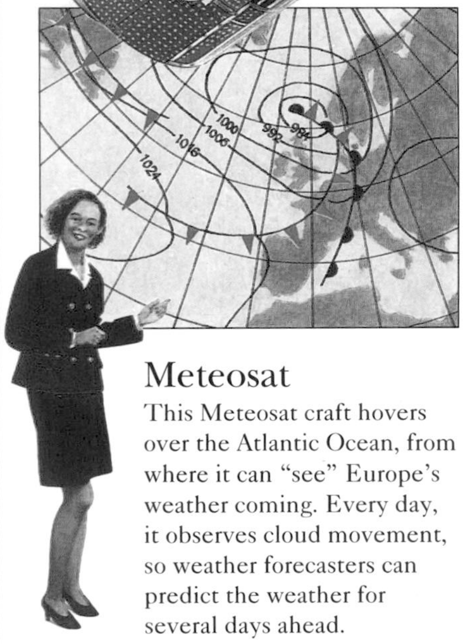

Meteosat

This Meteosat craft hovers over the Atlantic Ocean, from where it can "see" Europe's weather coming. Every day, it observes cloud movement, so weather forecasters can predict the weather for several days ahead.

Is anyone out there?

Radio telescopes on Earth are listening day and night for messages from space, but after almost 40 years, not one has been picked up! In 1974 we sent a message to a distant star cluster from Arecibo Observatory, Puerto Rico, the world's biggest radio telescope. It will be the 270th century before it gets there, and the 520th century before we could receive a reply!

"Sorry, wrong galaxy!"

Pioneer 10

The space probe Pioneer 10 was the first spacecraft to cross the asteroid belt and fly past Jupiter. It is now 15.6 billion km (9.7 billion miles) from Earth. Every day it travels 536,000 km (334,000 miles) into space.

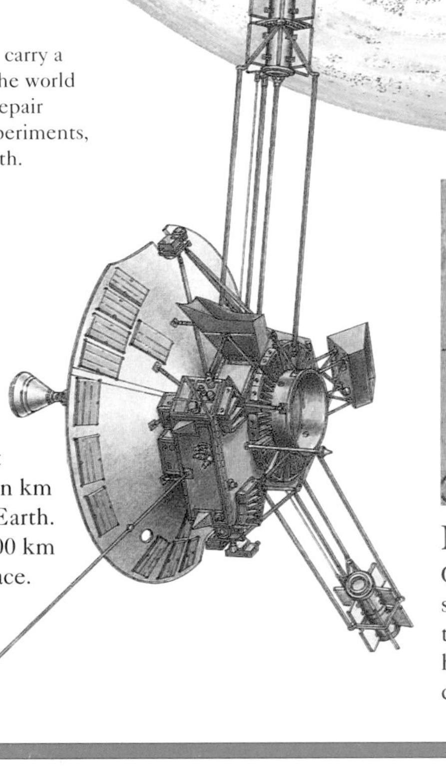

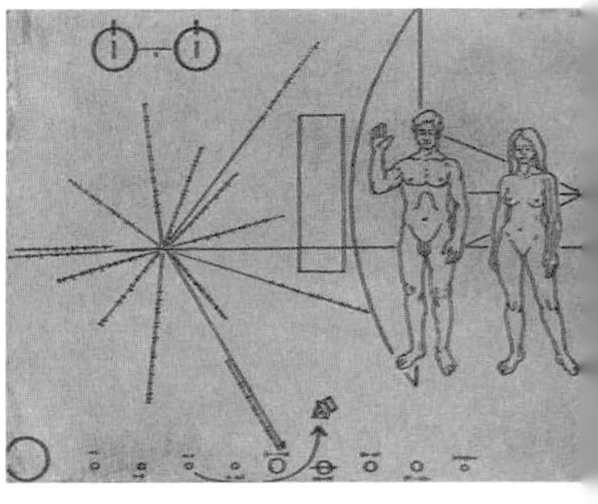

Message to other worlds

On its side, Pioneer 10 carries a plaque showing human figures and a diagram c the Earth's position in the Universe. It hoped that one day aliens will find the craft and communicate with Earth.

Letters from America

The world sends 1.2 billion letters through the post every day. If all these letters could be stacked together, they would make a bridge that would span the Atlantic Ocean.

USA
The USA handles 603 million items of mail in one day.

UK
The UK handles around 50 million items of mail a day – that's one letter every day for each of the inhabitants of the British Isles.

With love from me to you

Christmas Day is celebrated in the USA with 2.7 billion festive cards. One million romantic Americans lick stamps to catch the post for Valentine's Day on 14 February.

SMALL WORLD

The Pentagon, Arlington, Virginia, is the headquarters of the American Department of Defense. It has one of the world's largest private telephone systems, with 34,500 individual lines, handling a million calls a day. It also has the world's largest pneumatic tube system, with 24 km (15 miles) of tube, through which letters are transported by means of air pressure.

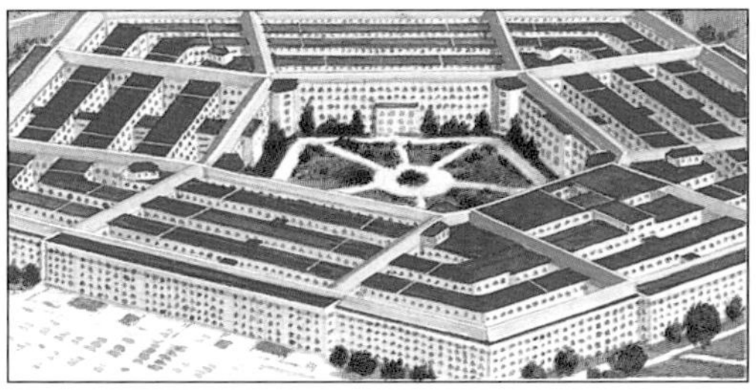

HALCA
This Japanese radio astronomy satellite travels around Earth four times every day.

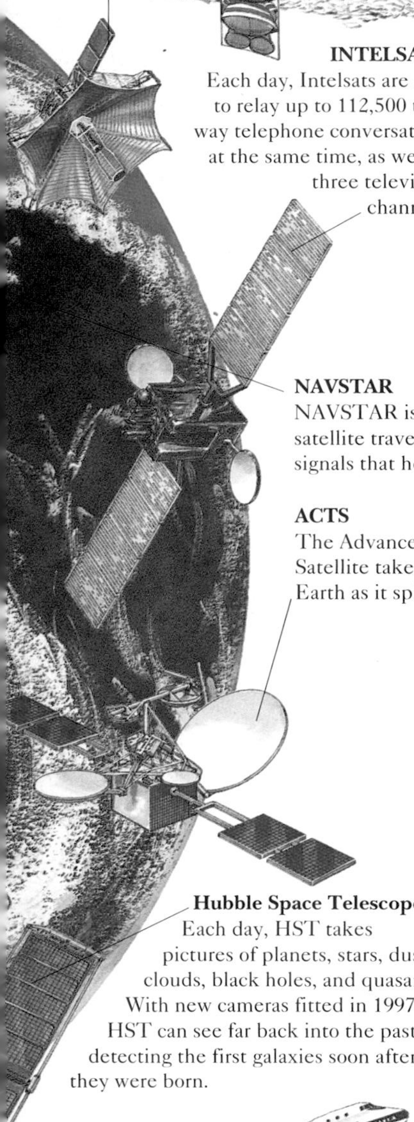

INTELSAT 8
Each day, Intelsats are able to relay up to 112,500 two-way telephone conversations at the same time, as well as three television channels.

NAVSTAR
NAVSTAR is a series of 24 navigation satellites. Each satellite travels around the Earth twice a day, sending signals that help boats and planes to locate their positions.

ACTS
The Advanced Communications Technology Satellite takes exactly 24 hours to orbit the Earth as it spins on its axis.

Hubble Space Telescope
Each day, HST takes pictures of planets, stars, dust clouds, black holes, and quasars. With new cameras fitted in 1997, HST can see far back into the past, detecting the first galaxies soon after they were born.

"Any more glue and I'll get lockjaw!"

Stampede

Americans lick around 13.7 million stamps every day. Pasted edge to edge, they would cover two American football fields.

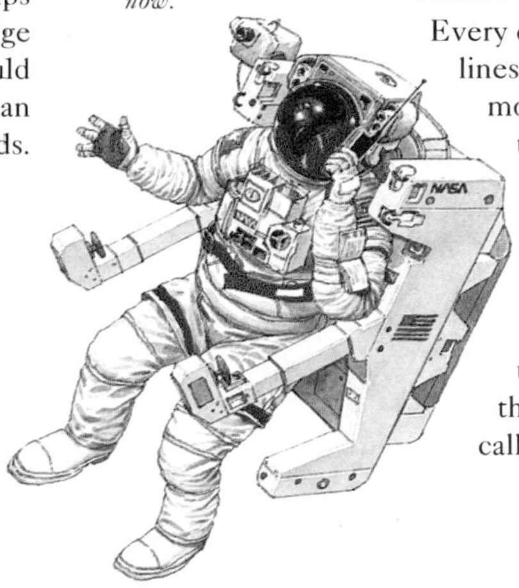
"I'm out of the country right now."

'Allo? 'Allo?

Every day, 652 million telephone lines and more than 100 million mobile phones are in use across the world. Most of the talking goes on in North America. The average American makes five calls a day. If the total daily calls between the USA and Canada were added up into a single conversation, they would make a telephone call 23 years long!

"Your Shuttle needs servicing, mate."

"Salut!"
"Hello!"
"Bore da!"
"Jambo!"
"Iska warran!"
"Hej!"
"Ciao!"
"Dumela!"
"Hoi!"
"Alo!"
"Kumusta!"

Lots of chat

Every day, people around the world communicate with each other in thousands of different languages, each with its own culture and traditions.

Computer-speak

Computers were first used for communications in 1969 by scientists and academics. Now, people in 150 countries around the globe talk to each other every day on the Internet.

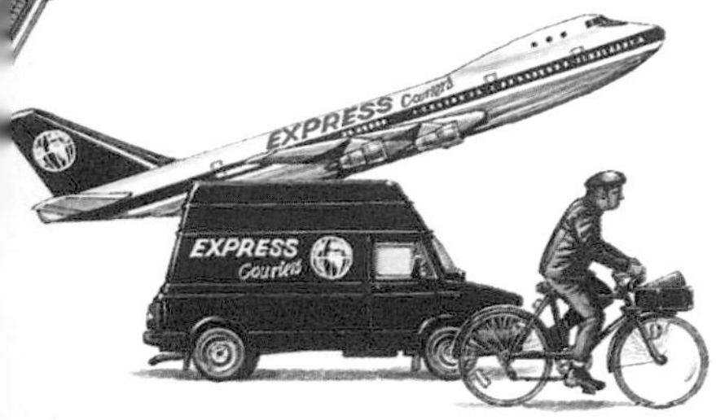

Don't shoot the messenger

Every business day, Federal Express delivers more than two million items to over 200 countries around the world.

"Bloomin' bootiful!"

Flower power

Every day, the British communicate happiness, sympathy, or regret by sending 11,000 bunches of flowers.

A DAY TO REMEMBER

Dots and dashes

On 8 January 1838, the first Morse Code message was sent by a student of Samuel Morse. It read: "A patient waiter is no loser."

Altitude problem

The biro was patented on 10 June 1943 by László Josef Biró. It was used by navigators, as fountain pens leak at altitude, and pencils do not mark weatherproof maps.

Royal cable

On 16 August 1858, Queen Victoria sent a formal greeting to American President James Buchanan. She was the first head of state to use the world's first transatlantic cable.

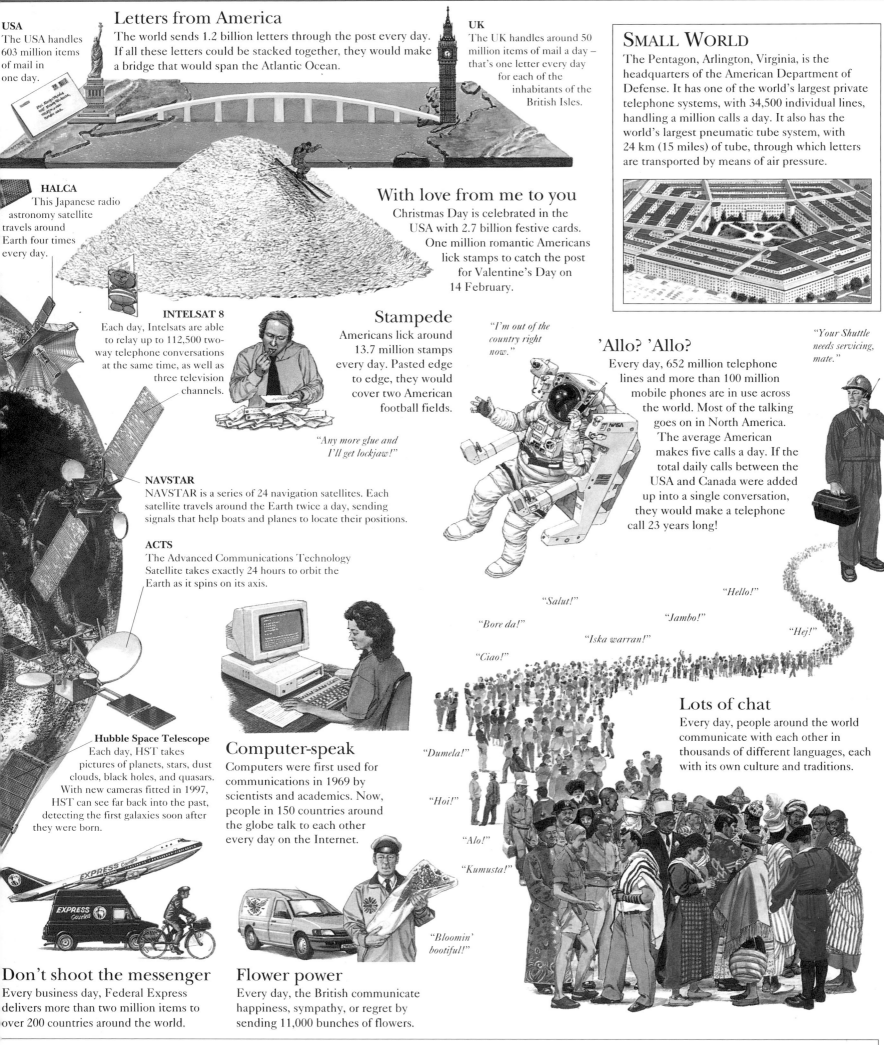

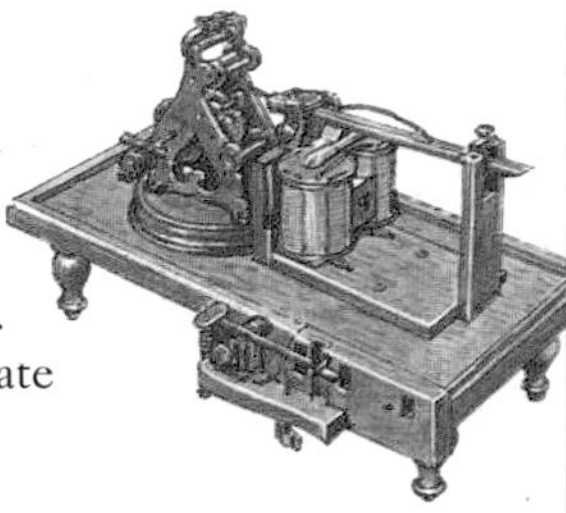

TRAVEL

IF ALL THE FOOTSTEPS TAKEN IN THE WORLD in one day could be put together to make one long journey, the human race could walk 88 times to the Sun and back every 24 hours. On wheels, wings, water, and on its feet, this restless world is constantly on the move. Travelling is more comfortable for some than for others. In the West, there is a car for every two people. In Ethiopia, there is only one car for every 1,468 people.

World flights

Every day there are 45,000 scheduled flights carrying more than 3.5 million passengers. This is equivalent to the total population of Puerto Rico taking to the skies.

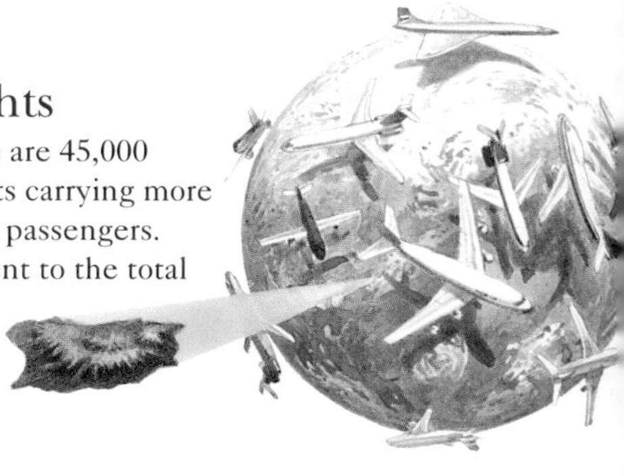

On the go all day

How far could the different forms of transport in this fleet travel in a day if each one maintained its maximum cruising speed over 24 hours? In reality, of course, fuel tanks would run dry, engines would overheat, and stamina would flag long before the day was out.

Gas balloon
Travels at 16 kph (10 mph). In 24 hours, it could cover 384 km (240 miles).

Passenger helicopter
Cruises at 241 kph (150 mph). In 24 hours, it could travel 5,784 km (3,600 miles).

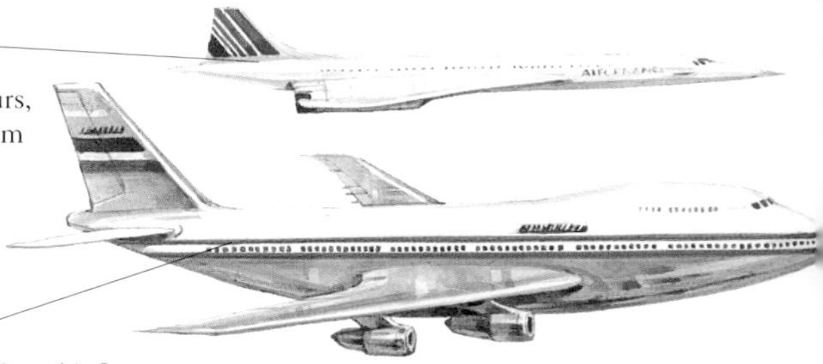

Concorde
Cruises at 2,222 kph (1,450 mph). In 24 hours, it could cover 53,328 km (34,800 miles).

Boeing 747-400
Cruises at 901 kph (560 mph). In 24 hours, it could travel 21,624 km (13,440 miles).

SeaCat ferry
Cruises at 64 kph (40 mph). In 24 hours it could cover 1,536 km (960 miles).

Hovercraft
Travels at 120 kph (75 mph). In 24 hours, it could cover 2,880 km (1,800 miles).

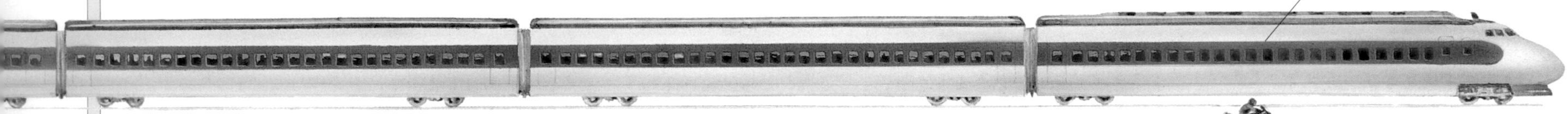

Japanese Series E2 train
Cruises at 275 kph (171 mph). In 24 hours, it could cover 6,600 km (4,104 miles).

Motorbike
Can cruise at 129 kmh (80 mph). In 24 hours it could cover 3,096 km (1,920 miles).

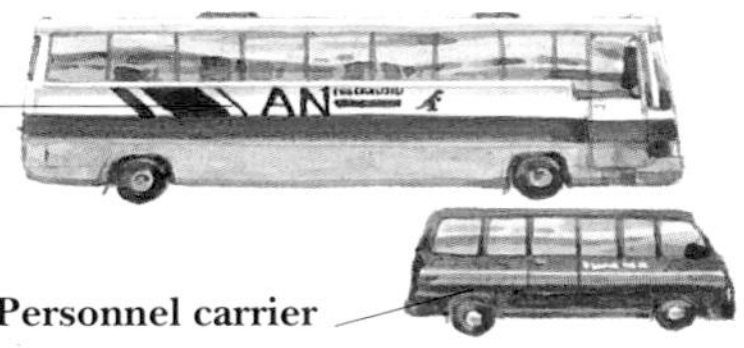

European coach and personnel carrier
Both these vehicles can cruise along the motorway at 113 kph (70 mph). In 24 hours they would cover 2,712 km (1,680 miles).

Personnel carrier

Heathrow Airport

London Heathrow has more international passengers than any other airport in the world. On an average day, it handles 105,000 passengers, 2,000 tonnes of freight – which might include racing cars and racehorses, as well as exotic fruit and vegetables – and 200 tonnes of mail. Every day, 1,200 aircraft land and take off. The airport's busiest day so far was 30 June 1995, when 194,500 passengers passed through it.

Every day, Heathrow has 36 flights to Paris and 22 flights to New York.

Every day, 35,000 of Heathrow's passengers travel on to a further destination.

93 different airlines operate at Heathrow

Heathrow's cafés and bars sell 26,000 cups of tea and coffee, 6,500 pints of beer and 6,500 sandwiches every day.

Each aircraft holds an average of 130 passengers.

156,000 items of baggage pass through Heathrow Airport every day.

Every day, 40–50 Very Important Persons get special treatment as they pass through the airport.

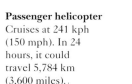

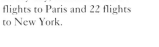

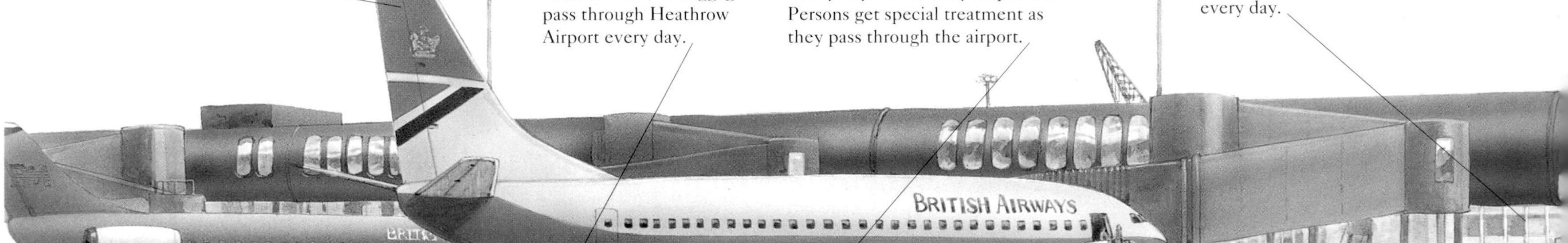

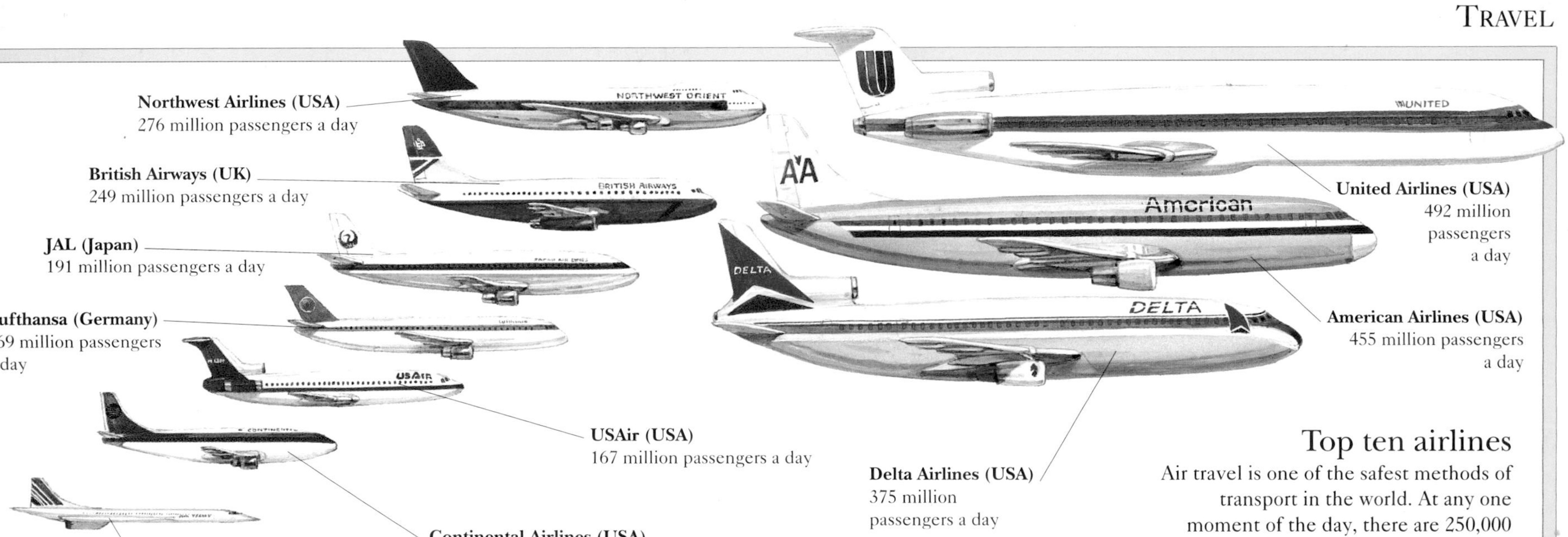

Top ten airlines

Air travel is one of the safest methods of transport in the world. At any one moment of the day, there are 250,000 people up in the air in planes.

A DAY TO REMEMBER

Sir Clive's car

On 10 January 1985, British inventor Sir Clive Sinclair launched his battery-powered vehicle. It was a commercial disaster.

Biggest jam

The world's worst traffic jam happened on 16 February 1980, on the road from Paris to Lyons, France. Traffic was at a standstill for a staggering 176 km (109 miles).

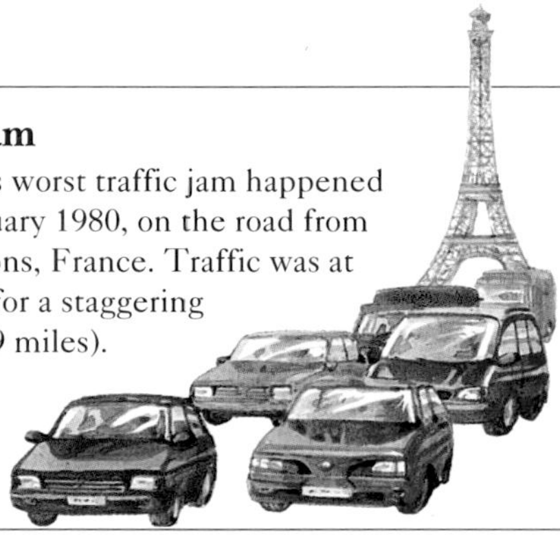

Broken down

The worst day for car breakdowns in the UK was 2 January 1996, when the Automobile Association and Royal Automobile Club came to the aid of 41,670 motorists.

All the traffic in the world

There are 480 million cars and 150 million commercial vehicles in the world. If they all went out at the same time, they could form a six-lane traffic jam to the Moon.

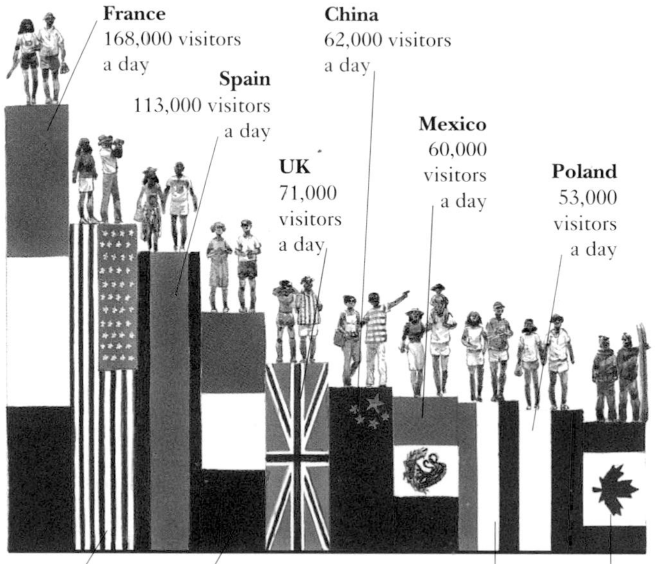

Top ten destinations

Every day, 1.6 million people visit the world's top ten tourist countries. More than 10 per cent of the world's travellers head for France every day.

Passports

Every day, 3 million passports are checked at airports and border crossings over the world. If they were stacked up on top of one another, the pile would be 9 km (5.6 miles) high, taller than Mount Everest.

ery day, 80,000 ple work at athrow Airport, or rby in jobs that vice its smooth ration.

275 birds, 275 reptiles, and 137 mammals, including 15 cats and dogs pass through Heathrow Airport each day. Airline cargo compartments in which animals travel are temperature-controlled and pressurized for their wellbeing.

40 air traffic controllers work shifts around the clock to ensure the safety of planes during take-off and landing.

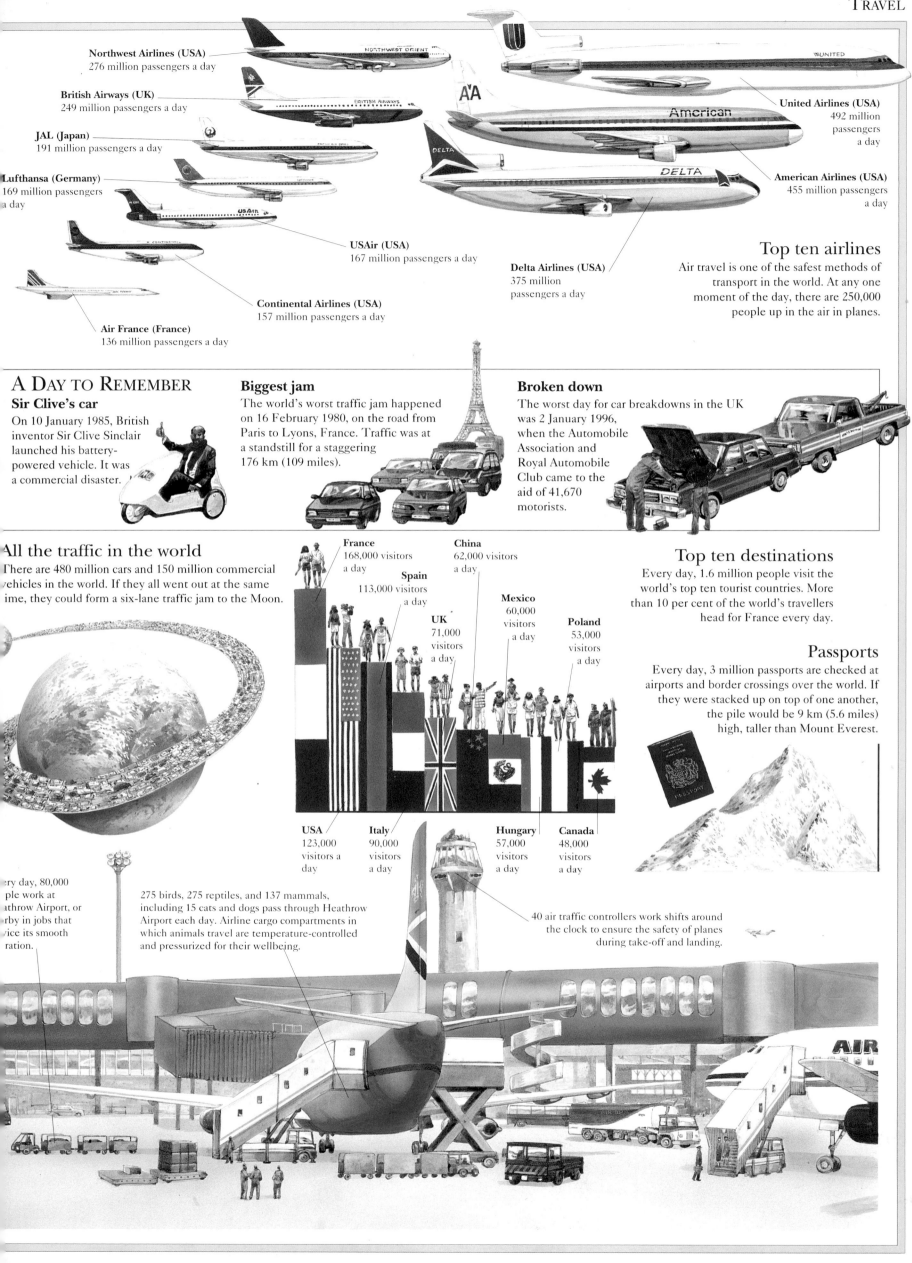

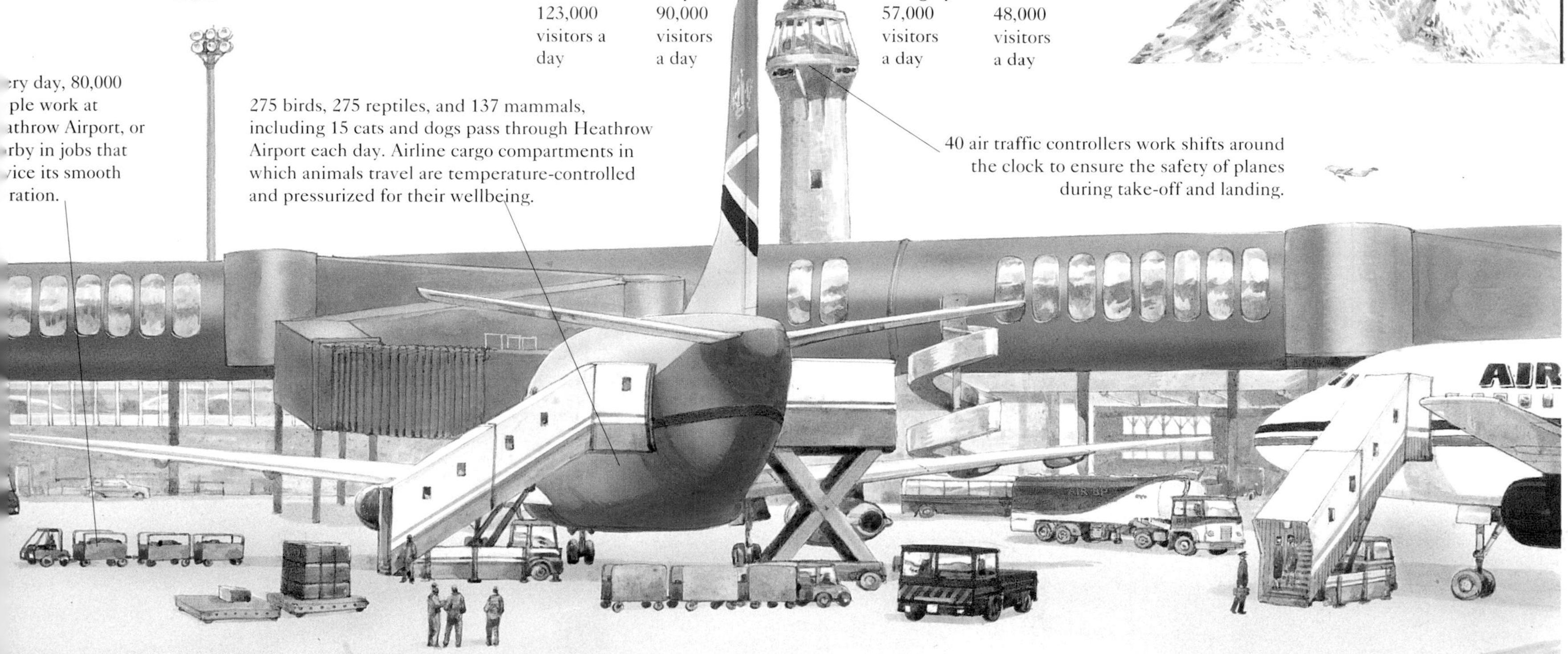

A DAY OFF

WHAT DO YOU DO when you have time to yourself? Do you spring into action and ride off on your bike, or put on your in-line skates? Or do you do as little as possible and simply sit down in front of the TV, or sing in the bath? Do you want to be thrilled and entertained at a theme park or at the cinema? Do you travel the world and marvel at its wonders, from the mighty Grand Canyon to the Great Pyramid? Whatever you do, you will be surprised to discover how many other people are spending the day doing it too!

The Grand Canyon, Arizona, USA, has 12,000 visitors a day.
The CN Tower, Toronto, Canada, attracts 5,000 visitors a day.
Kennedy Space Center, Florida, USA, sells 1,500 tickets to admit visitors to watch the launch of the Shuttle.
The Empire State Building, New York, USA, attracts 7,000 visitors a day.
The Blackpool Tower, Blackpool, UK, draws 3,300 visitors a day.
Ayers Rock, Northern Territory, Australia, has 900 visitors a day.
Stonehenge, Wiltshire, UK, attracts 2,000 visitors a day.
Kew Gardens, London, UK, has 2,700 visitors a day.
The Tower of London, London, UK, attracts 7,000 visitors a day.
The Eiffel Tower, Paris, France, attracts 15,000 visitors a day.
The Great Pyramid, Giza, Egypt, draws 10,000 visitors a day.
Old Faithful Geyser, Yellowstone National Park, USA, has 8,000 visitors a day.
Universal Studios, California, USA, draws 15,000 visitors a day.
The British Museum, London, UK, has 17,000 visitors a day.
The Louvre Museum, Paris, France, attracts 17,000 visitors every day.

A day out, a night out

All the world loves a day out. Every day, 173,000 people visit America's National Parks. The world's most spectacular night out is offered by Monte Carlo. Every night for a week in July and August each year, as part of an international competition, one tonne of fireworks are launched into the skies above the Mediterranean harbour.

French camping

The French have a passion for camping, and an abundance of beautiful countryside in which to pitch their tents. Every night, nearly 3 million French people sleep under canvas.

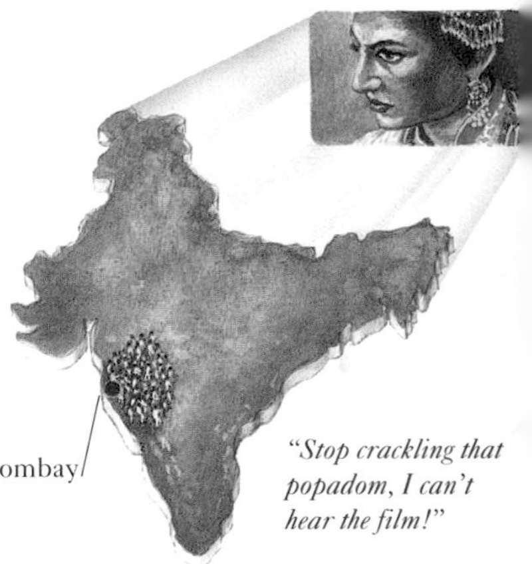

Bombay

"Stop crackling that popadom, I can't hear the film!"

Indian movies

India is the most film-loving nation in the world. It has 13,000 screens, including 4,000 mobile cinemas. Every day, 15 million Indians visit the movies. That's like having the whole population of Bombay, India's film-making capital, at the cinema.

Golf mad

The world has 28 million golfers. If they all went out on the same day, it would be like having the population of Tanzania on the golf course. There are more golfers per head of population in Japan than anywhere else in the world. Every day, 450,000 of them play golf on a course, and because space is limited in Japan, 850,000 Japanese thwack balls every day on indoor driving ranges.

"I'm gonna hit that ball all the way to Timbuktu."

New Zealand and Ireland 132,000 golfers

Scotland 220,000 golfers

Australia 374,000 golfers

England 495,000 golfers

Japan 8 million golfers

USA 18 million golfers

Golf balls

More than 820,000 golf balls are sold worldwide every day. More than half of them are bought by Japanese golfers!

A sporting nation

The Americans are the most health-conscious people in the world. Every day, millions of them puff and puff through energetic sports and exercise routines. For 70 million Americans, the favourite way of keeping trim and fit is to walk or jog. A staggering 30 million Americans participate in in-line skating.

60 million Americans get in the swim.
50 million Americans get on their bikes.
"What a sweat!"
44 million Americans lift weights or use other exercise equipment, in gyms or at home.
37 million Americans go bowling.
"Gotta get that ball in that net!"
28 million Americans play basketball.
10 million
20 million
30 million
40 million
50 million
60 million

Goggle-box lives

In many homes in the Western world, the glowing picture box at the heart of the house is hardly ever turned off. First there were TV dinners, then came breakfast-time TV. Now people who live TV lives can also shop and bank through the box.

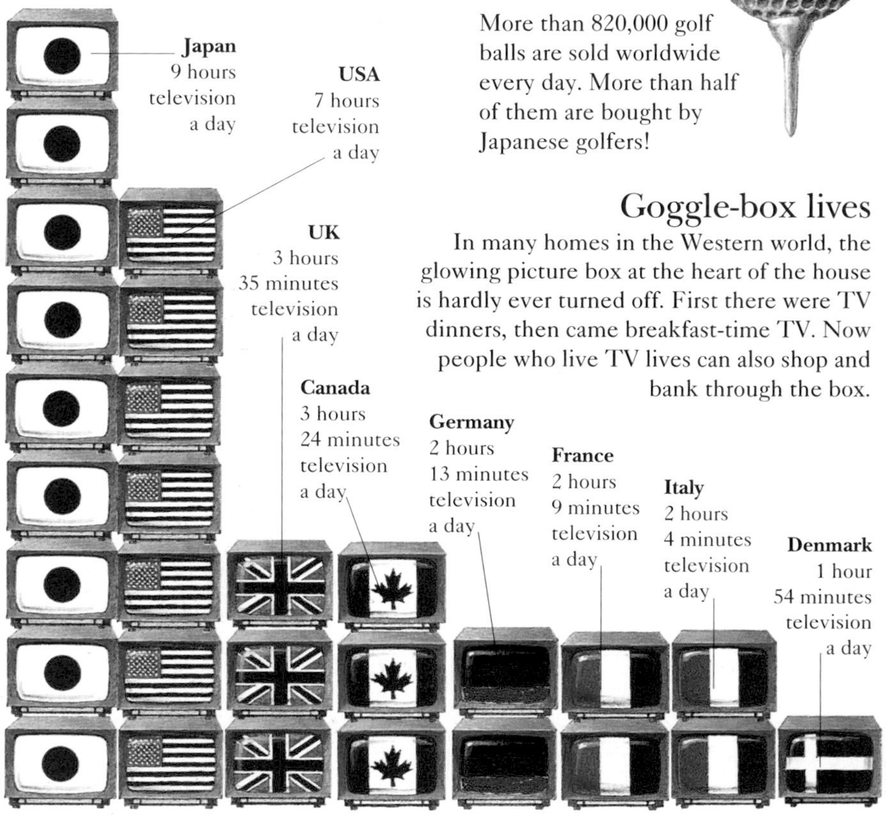
Japan 9 hours television a day
USA 7 hours television a day
UK 3 hours 35 minutes television a day
Canada 3 hours 24 minutes television a day
Germany 2 hours 13 minutes television a day
France 2 hours 9 minutes television a day
Italy 2 hours 4 minutes television a day
Denmark 1 hour 54 minutes television a day

A Day to Remember

Royal wedding

The biggest television audience ever – 750 million people around the world – tuned in to watch the wedding of the Prince and Princess of Wales on 29 July 1981. Two hundred and fifty million people listened on the radio and 500,000 lined the streets of London to watch the event live.

Carry on karaoke

Every day in Japan, 800,000 people sing karaoke in public. In the United States, more than 3 million recordings – including 2 million CDs – are sold in just one day. The UK sells 800,000 recordings a day.

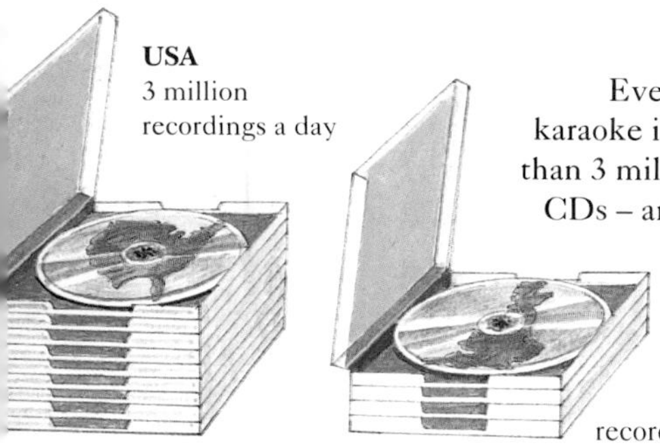

USA 3 million recordings a day

UK 800,000 recordings a day

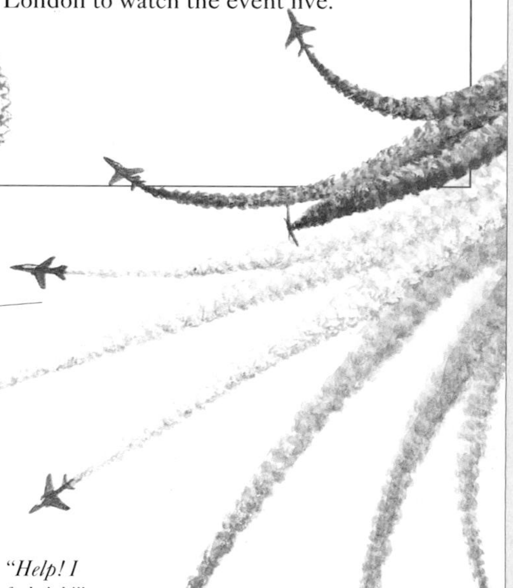
"Help! I feel sick!"

Paris Air Show, 326,000 visitors in one day. The air show takes place every two years in June.

Carnival, Rio de Janeiro, Brazil. 50,000 people parade through the streets in costume every day during the carnival.

Disneyland, Tokyo, Japan. 42,000 people visit the world's most popular Disneyland every day.

Niagara Falls, Canada/USA. Every day, 30,000 people visit the spectacular waterfalls.

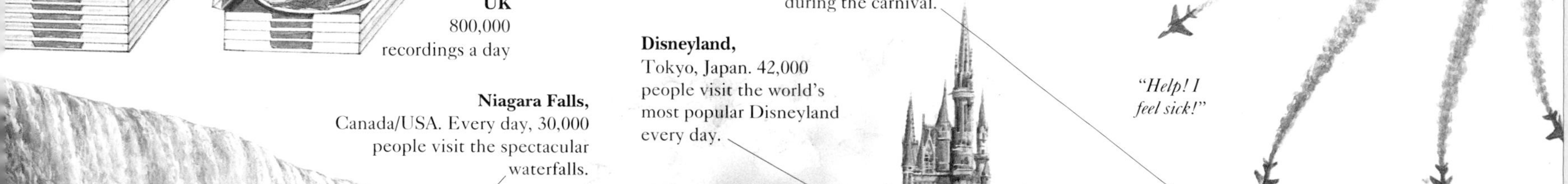

Index

Acknowledegments
Dorling Kindersley would like to thank the following people for helping with this book:
Illustrators: Richard Bonson, Stephen Conlin, Peter Dennis (Linda Rogers Associates), Chris Forsey, Malcolm Mcgregor and Peter Visscher.
Editorial: Francesca Baines, Robert Graham, Angela Koo, Nichola Roberts.
Design: Simon Faiers
Index: Chris Bernstein
Additional Acknowledgements: The Automobile Association, Biosphere II, Peter Bond, Gary Booth, Heathrow Airport, Kew Gardens, Keith Lye, Milton Keynes Recycling Facility, Royal Automobile Club, Royal Horticultural Society Library, Martin Walters, Richard Walters, World Resources Foundation.

Special thanks to Caroline Ash